"I drank down Mai'a Williams's *This Is How We Survive* like a glass of delicious water hitting me where I was the most thirsty. Williams gives us the story we've been waiting for and deeply needing, about the ways Black, Indigenous, and Brown women and mothers across the globe birth freedom struggle as they open their homes, hold late-night cigarette conversations, and insist that everyone be present to the work of liberation. Her work, and her life's story, is crucial to what will bring us home."
—Leah Lakshmi Piepzna-Samarasinha, writer and organizer, author of *Dirty River: A Queer Femme of Color Dreaming Her Way Home*

"In reading the work of Mai'a Williams, it's hard not to be excited by the sense of possibility."
—*Hip Mama*

"*This Is How We Survive* redefines revolution beyond the headline grabbing events to the everyday resilience of families living under ever-present threats of bombings, assaults, arrests, and disappearances. This book will push you to expand and reimagine your definitions and ideas of revolution."
—Victoria Law, author of *Resistance Behind Bars: The Struggles of Incarcerated Women*

This Is How We Survive

Revolutionary Mothering, War, and Exile in the 21st Century

This Is How We Survive: Revolutionary Mothering, War, and Exile in the 21st Century
Mai'a Williams
© 2019 PM Press.

ISBN: 978–1–62963–556–9
Library of Congress Control Number: 2018931529

Cover by John Yates / www.stealworks.com
Interior design by briandesign

10 9 8 7 6 5 4 3 2 1

PM Press
PO Box 23912
Oakland, CA 94623
www.pmpress.org

Printed in the USA by the Employee Owners of Thomson-Shore in Dexter, Michigan.
www.thomsonshore.com

Let me tell you a story about migration, about movement, the back and forth of love. Across boundaries and borders, across heartbreak and forgiveness. Let me tell you how we got free, got imprisoned, broke out, broke down, and got up to fight once again. Let me tell you about memory, about resistance, and yes about mothering. This is a story for these times. About what it takes to create love in the face of fascism. The war is everywhere. The war is here. And this is how we are going to survive the 21st century.

Contents

Foreword

When I first became a mother, my politicized communities back in the United States frowned on the whole thing like it was a sellout to consumerist normalcy. Revolution, they believed, was fought in the streets with no concern for the babies on our backs or the underpaid babysitters at our apartments or the multigenerational conversations that happened over dinner-making.

This kind of thinking hasn't gotten us very far.

We don't need angry masculinity to fight angry masculinity. We don't need the mind-sets of colonialism and enslavement to save us from the genocidal legacies of colonialism and enslavement.

So what's the real alternative to this shit-show of a white capitalist war machine? Maybe it starts with centering femmes, mothers, and children. Welcome to Mai'a Williams's revolutionary love experiment, a dynamic test kitchen of radical reenvisioning that will affirm, inspire, and transform the way you think about and engage in parenting, direct action, and self-preservation.

At turns empowered in her defiance and plowed over by cops and doctors, our mama-guide through these pages never claims to have all the answers, but she's willing to take us along on the learning curve. Because this is real life, and time is of the essence.

These are stories of real revolutions blooming every day in everyday communities all over the world. These are stories of femmes, mothers, and children centering each other. This is the resistance we don't see on TV.

In times of quickening instability, Mai'a knows that it's easy to feel overwhelmed, to succumb to the fears that late-stage capitalism feeds on, to get depressed. And it's not that she doesn't feel these ways sometimes—it's just that she insists on living and standing up to power anyway.

When she meets a mother in eastern Democratic Republic of Congo who envisions a society that would reward her sons for working toward the good of the community and not for destroying the community, Mai'a's ethos, the ethos of this book, crystalizes: We are talking about moral liberation here. We are talking about centering love instead of greed.

Mai'a does it the way Mai'a does it. This book will have you strategizing ways to do it the ways you'll do it. Because this is how we survive. It's ancient and brand new. It's radical love. It's the kind of revolution that multigenerational, politicized communities everywhere are ready for.

Ariel Gore

Some Thoughts on Revolutionary Love and Survival in the 21st Century

There is no end
To what a living world
Will demand of you
                    —Octavia Butler

I've been accused of being impatient. It's true. I'm impatient. I don't have time to fuck around. None of us do. There is hard work to be done now. And those of us on the margins—we mamas, caretakers, femmes, black aunties, lovers, and fighters—the work is on us. It's not fair that this work is on us, but it is. No one else is going to do it.

Have you seen white people for the past five hundred years, their colonization and enslavements, their genocides and exploitation of the natural world? The delusions they tell themselves that they are somehow so separate from the natural world, that they can destroy the world, each other, and us and—still survive? They are a mess.

They have, decade after decade, century after century, become so morally and rationally weak that they have convinced themselves that two minus two equals infinity, not zero. That greed is good. That the earth is flat. That the heart doesn't break at death. That love is slave work, roses, and complacency. That heaven is what we gain once they make hell on earth.

These are not people we can rely on to save us from themselves. They are still burning the earth away.

In 2005, when I was in the eastern Democratic Republic of Congo (DRC), I met with communities of mamas who were doing the hard, life-giving work of recreating civil society in the midst of wars. The Congolese farmer women told me that they can't predict the weather anymore. Clouds don't mean what they used to. And their children are taken to the mines to dig coltan so that we can have smartphones.

> *The consequences of the globalized world economy would certainly have been far more nefarious except for the efforts that millions of women have made to ensure that their families would be supported, regardless of their value on the capitalist labor market. Through their subsistence activities, as well as various forms of direct action (from squatting on public land to urban farming) women have helped their communities to avoid total dispossession, to extend budgets and add food to the kitchen pots. Amid wars, economic crises, and devaluations, as the world around them was falling apart, they have planted corn on abandoned town plots, cooked food to sell on the side of the streets, created communal kitchens—ola communes, as in Chile and Peru—thus standing in the way of a total commodification of life and beginning a process of re-appropriation and re-collectivization of reproduction that is indispensable if we are to regain control over our lives.*
> —Silvia Federici

We all are implicated in late-stage capitalism. And yes, some folks are much more implicated and responsible than others. If we survive into the 22nd century, there will need to be some reckoning. Someday we will need a truth-and-reconciliation commission where the descendants of thieves don't get to keep the wealth.

But first we need to survive. And that's on all of us.

I used to believe that revolution could save us. That revolution, deep social transformation that centers the work and needs of the least among us, could stop the death machines. That we, humans and nonhumans, conquerors and conquered, would come together and find a way to live, in justice, peace and harmony, to restore the earth and waters and soil. That we would be able to stop this madness. But lately when I read environmental reports, I hear the alarms of scientists ringing. And I realize they have grown more desperate. Scientists used to tell us what was going to happen if we didn't stop this madness. Now they just tell us what level of annihilation is coming into being: earthquakes in South Carolina, desertification in Yemen, and ancient diseases finding new life. And yes, the earth has always changed, but this is happening all too fast.

I'm not saying that resistance isn't still possible, I'm just wondering if resistance is enough. At best, a revolution might make it possible that more of us who love and care for the water and life will survive this century. But I still believe in revolution.

In large part, my writing is inspired by the mamas I met and talked with over the years. Conversations about childcare and burnout, fathers and grandmothers, schools, poems, tea, music, activism, and good cheap takeout food. The laughter and the overwhelming expectations, the fear and the rituals of living. How we make life out of no life. How we make life out of our own lives. How we make life.

> *Globalization aims to give corporate capital total control over labor and natural resources. Thus it must expropriate workers from any means of subsistence that may enable them to resist a more intense exploitation. As such it cannot succeed except through a systematic attack on the material conditions of social reproduction and on the main subjects of this work, which in most countries are women.*
>
> *Women are also victimized because they are guilty of the two main crimes which globalization is supposed to combat. They are the ones who, with their struggles, have*

contributed most to "valorizing" the labor of their children and communities, challenging the sexual hierarchies on which capitalism has thrived and forcing the nation state to expand investment in the reproduction of the workforce. They have also been the main supporters of a noncapitalist use of natural resources (lands, waters, forests) and subsistence-oriented agriculture, and therefore have stood in the way of both the full commercialization of "nature" and the destruction of the last remaining commons.

—Silvia Federici

Science Fiction

There seem to be solid biological reasons why we are the way we are. If there weren't, the cycles wouldn't keep replaying. The human species is a kind of animal, of course. But we can do something no other animal species has ever had the option to do. We can choose: We can go on building and destroying until we either destroy ourselves or destroy the ability of our world to sustain us. Or we can make something more of ourselves.

—Octavia Butler

I've stopped taking it all so personally. The racism and capitalism and ecocide, the sexism and homophobia, how tired everyone in the United States seems even though they claim they are living the best life in the best country in the world. When folks are being worked to the bone and drinking poisoned water in their coffee every morning, there isn't a lot of psychological energy left to figure out that this "best life" is all a hoax and a wink. I imagine that anti-Blackness and capitalism and ableism are huge mindless machines with tentacles hooked into people's spines, making them unable to stand for what is right. Every day I pray, not for the revolution, not for a savior, just to have the strength to constantly disentangle myself from the machine.

Science fiction creators taught me not to take the machine personally: the wear and tear, day in and day out, of micro-aggressions and weird looks and empty bank accounts, and off-conversations and news reports and movies and some drunk guy trying to holla at me and another cop found not guilty for shooting a Black boy who wasn't even old enough to vote, and our water tasting like rusty metal. While we do need to constantly unplug from the violence of the invisible machines, we aren't going to survive simply by boycotting products made in Israeli settlements or having multiracial babies. We aren't going to survive by "voting with our dollars," and we aren't going to make a revolution through the purity of our lifestyles.

We Are Not the Ones Destroying the Earth

Marginalized mothers—poor mothers, queer mothers, single mothers, Black and Brown mothers, Native mothers, teen mothers, etc.—we mamas are the ones who are often blamed by mainstream discourse for the economic destruction and ecological degradation that is happening to this planet and human communities. We are blamed for the very collapse of societies globally. We are not the ones destroying the earth.

For many of us, the end of the world happened a long time ago. For many Native folks in the Americas, the end of the world began five hundred years ago. For the colonized folks on the African continent, the end of the world, the nearly whole-sale ecological and economic destruction, has taken place, is taking place. No need for the future tense when the apocalypse has already happened to us.

And yet, the end of rapacious and murderous Western civilization, the global North, is blamed on mothers. Poor mothers are depicted as welfare queens living off the teat of the government and "hardworking" taxpayers. Queer mothers and single mothers are destroying the very foundation of the nuclear family. Black mothers can only reproduce criminality. Immigrant mothers are just producing anchor babies and are destroying the very concept of what "nationhood" and "nation-state" mean.

First, good on these mothers for doing the work of destroying oppressive structures such as nation-statehood, the nuclear heteronormative family, and for redistributing money and resources from the wealthy and the government coffers back to the poor, Indigenous, and colonized, so that these folks have the opportunity to create more liberated and egalitarian community structures.

Second, and more importantly, marginalized mamas are not destroying the fabrics that support us as whole human beings. We are not the ones destroying the earth. We are not the ones creating civil wars that kill millions of people and create droughts and famines in east Africa. We are not the reason that there are refugee crises happening in Syria, Yemen, and South Sudan. We did not cause the global recession in 2008. No, that was caused by banks too big to fail and decades of economic policies that allowed for speculative finance to run wild. We are not the reason that there still isn't clean water in Flint, Michigan. We aren't the reason that a massive chunk of iceberg, nearly the size of Delaware, broke off Antarctica's Larsen Ice Shelf recently. We did not cause global warming and climate instability. We are not the ones destroying the earth, we are liberatory, resistance communities that are humanity's best chance for humans and nonhumans to survive into the next century.

> *What is needed is the reopening of a collective struggle over reproduction, reclaiming control over the material conditions of our reproduction and creating new forms of cooperation around this work outside of the logic of capital and market. This is not a utopia, but a process already under way in many parts of the world and likely to expand in the face of a collapse of the world financial system. Governments are now attempting to use the crisis*

to impose stiff austerity regimes on us for years to come.
But through land takeovers, urban farming, community-
supported agriculture, through squats, the creation of
various forms of barter, mutual aid, alternative forms of
healthcare—to name some of the terrains on which the
reorganization of reproduction is more developed—a new
economy is beginning to emerge that may turn reproduc-
tive work from a stifling, discriminating activity into the
most liberating and creative ground of experimentation
in human relations.

—Silvia Federici

Mothering isn't gendered. Everyone, including and especially men, must engage in this mothering work. Like Alice Walker says, "Mothering is an instinct, yes, but it is also a practice. It can be learned." I go further and say it should be learned. Mothering is the only way we are going to survive into the 22nd century. And we have to center those who are most skilled in that work, many of whom are mothers of children. Some of us have been socialized, trained, in this work. This is our best chance for saving the human species and all living beings from annihilation.

In every community I've worked with, it was mamas who actually held it down. They continue to be the locus of strategy for resisting the genocidal powers that be. Mamas are going to survive because mamas create families, communities, relationships, and new ecologies that are rooted in humanity's survival. New ways of loving each other. A new world of liberation and justice, of local control over land and resources, of anti-violence, of new economies being created outside of capitalistic control.

These new/old ways of being exist everywhere in the third world. People sitting on worn blankets and selling goods, foods, and services on the side of the road. Community, mutual aid, local gardens, folks squatting empty buildings, and recreating homes and sites of production and reproduction. They are hair-braiders and marijuana dealers, herbalists and traditional healers, sex workers and cooks selling empanadas out of their makeshift kitchen windows. These new communities of sharing, bartering, and trading, of creating local currencies, are being reproduced daily by women. By mothers. By mother of mothers. We are the ones learning new ways to love and thrive.

We create resistance communities and safe spaces not just for the little nuclear families, but for all the lovers and fighters, so that we can rest, gather resources, and make connections between people and organizations engaged in this revolutionary work. Spaces set up all over the cities, mountains, jungles, and countrysides. This is the mothering work that makes the revolution possible.

But most activists brag about being out in the streets, not at home, making food and laughing, keeping first-aid kits stocked in the bathroom, and extra sheets and blankets for unexpected guests.

Mothering is revolutionary. Revolution is mothering. Revolution is impossible without mothering. And as Cynthia Oka said, there is no revolution without mothering.

> *For we have seen that, as soon as the anticolonial, the civil rights, and the feminist movements forced the system to make concessions, it reacted with the equivalent of a nuclear war. . . . If the destruction of our means of subsistence is indispensable for the survival of capitalist relations, this must be our terrain of struggle.*
> —Silvia Federici

When You Can't Opt Out of Revolution

> *The only way to survive is by taking care of one another.*
> —Grace Lee Boggs

In the global North, we have created radical activist communities that not only don't center radical mothering and caretaking but also push mothering, mamas, and children to the margins.

On the left, I hear conversations around mothers and children, and it is often in the context of how children and their mothers, disabled folks and their caretakers, would "get in the way" of the "real" activism work. Folks say the obligation of caretakers is to ensure the ultimate "safety" for children in movement work. They need to stay home, stay back. That those who are most physically and politically vulnerable should not be at the center or the front lines of our movements.

How did we forget that it is mamas and their children who are the impetus for our radical movements? It was Native youth who began the #NoDAPL movement at Standing Rock. Mamas in the eastern DRC are creating civil societies in the face of militant, political, and sexual violence. Youth in the West Bank are on the front lines of the uprisings. Mamas created the strategies and tactics that opposed the annihilation and genocide of Palestinians.

Back in the day, I worked in Palestinian communities, in which children were the targets of the Israeli military. I walked with Palestinian children to school past violent Israeli settlements and army checkpoints. These children couldn't and didn't opt out of the Intifada, the years and decades of uprising. They couldn't opt out of the revolution even though they were incredibly vulnerable. Their lives were on the line just to be educated. Just to go to school.

Egyptian youth went to the Cairo streets and demanded the fall of the regime. At Tahrir Square, mamas provided food, blankets, and childcare. They carried their young children on their shoulders to Tahrir Square while waving Egyptian flags and demanding "bread, freedom, and dignity." In the early days of the uprising, mothers and their kids celebrated, built community, and provided care for each other.

This was not what folks saw on the evening international news.

Without mothers and children, not just at the margins or the center of the revolution, but as the very context of revolution, who is left? Is it just a bunch of boys in black hoodies yelling on the front lines?

Dreams of a Moral Liberation

> *Freedom is not something that anybody can be given; freedom is something people take and people are as free as they want to be.*
>
> —James Baldwin

> *The function of freedom is to free someone else.*
>
> —Toni Morrison

When I was in the eastern Democratic Republic of Congo, in a small border town called Uvira, I talked with a woman community leader. When I asked her what her vision was, her hope for her community, she replied, "I want a moral liberation for my communities."

"What does 'moral liberation' mean?" I asked.

She said it was a society that would reward her sons for working toward the good of the community, because right now they were rewarded for destroying the community.

Before this conversation, I had spent two weeks listening to personal testimonies and community stories about the wars in the eastern DRC. Militias paid a pittance to boys and young men to massacre and rape their neighbors. Ever since I left the Congo, I've held onto this framework of morally liberatory communities: to be so free that we can act for the good of our community, of our humanity.

Moral liberatory praxis is the foundation of effective resistance and revolutionary communities. The work of mothering, of affirming life, is creating morally liberatory worlds and movements. It creates worlds where the act of mothering is supported and creates communities strong enough to resist the powers of colonization, of enslavement, of evil.

In every community I've worked in, I've seen that we aren't creating mothering communities; we aren't creating communities that center caretaking. That is, our primary work is not taking care of each other. And because of this we are not strengthening each other, and we aren't focused on working towards the good of the community.

Mothering isn't being supported. Mothers aren't themselves being mothered. And then we wonder why we don't have strong communities.

Revolution Will Break Your Heart

We are at one of the great turning points in human history when the survival of our planet and the restoration of our humanity require a great sea change in our ecological, economic, political, and spiritual values.

—Grace Lee Boggs

Only to the extent that we expose ourselves over and over to annihilation can that which is indestructible be found in us.

—Pema Chödrön

I watched the Egyptian revolution destroy itself. The daily work that created Tahrir Square and other resistance encampment sites in the Arab world became devalued by many activists. The work of "collective reproduction and cooperation" was falling apart.

In Palestine, I learned that revolutionary movements are not a one-time event, but a daily process, one of doing the sometimes-tiring, often-unglamorous work of nurturing the movement, by taking care of one another and ourselves. And often the benefits of this work to our personal self-interest, at least in the short term, are not evident.

Most movements I've witnessed or read about, over time, transform from the difficult, intricate work of caretaking and building community to the easy and flashy work of martyrs and heroes. The leadership, the loudest voices, take the daily work of sustaining revolutionary communities for granted. The life-affirming work of movement building are no longer centered and we watch movements break apart. Rather than supporting and deepening their commitments in practical and ideological ways to the Black feminist realization that "the personal is political," movement leadership often cleave the personal from the political, operating as if the personal and political exist in two separate realms, separate and definitely not equal.

Audre Lorde said we can learn to mother ourselves. I highly doubt the answer is that each of us takes care of ourselves first and then reaches out to take care of the other. I intuit that often we need to take care of the other so that we can learn and relearn to take care ourselves. Yes, we can learn to mother each other and, by doing so, we learn to mother ourselves. And simultaneously, by mothering ourselves, we can learn to mother each other.

Often when people proclaim that they have to take care of themselves first, especially by those who have so little practice at mothering, it simply becomes an excuse to indulge in individualism, claiming that self-centeredness is revolutionary.

The reproduction of revolutionary encampments and movements requires the centering of mothering and mothers. Starting from there, we build an ethos and praxis of resistance to the powers that be. Without mothering, revolution will tear us apart.

Revolution isn't an aesthetic. It isn't just an intellectual stance. It isn't tear gas and a beer. It is the daily discipline of justice. It is taking care of oneself and the other. It is creating the space to create just resistance communities.

I've watched people, time and again, try to calculate if they should extend emotional labor, see an issue or a situation as "their problem" by trying to figure out what were they going to personally gain. What was the immediate gain? The "that's not my problem" syndrome. And if they couldn't see an immediate gain versus the risk of what they would lose (time, maybe money, maybe prestige or social or professional status), then they didn't want to engage. This is often described as smart or strategic, but in reality it is counterrevolutionary.

But I get it because, honestly, revolution is scary and I fear it's still not enough to make a good world. Tremendous changes in all strata of one's life, situations, and conditions. The only way we are going to be able to ride and survive these changes without reverting back to oppressive lives and community structures is to build trust among each other. To take care of one another. To understand and practice revolutionary love as a long-term strategy. Immediate losses probably are necessary, if we are to recreate the world in the vision of justice, dignity, and life. "The arc of history is long," as Martin Luther King Jr. said, "but it bends toward justice," but only if we are willing to push the arc in that direction. This is the work.

When the mothering workers become burned out due to little to no compensation or acknowledgment, then the movement falls apart. And so many folks who didn't even notice who was doing the work run around with a thousand theories on why the revolution failed. To my heart, it seems obvious. Revolutionary love is the emotional labor in service to revolutionary movements. And we need revolutionary love in order to have a revolution.

Without mothering, revolution will break our hearts and break us apart because the heart of revolution is mothering.

Our Survival

This book is not a testament to me living out some revolutionary mothering dream or ideal. It is a book about my failures and successes, this experiment called revolution, this experiment called mothering.

I don't have all the answers or even most of them. My daughter can attest to that. I have some hunches, some inklings about how we who truly care about mamas and justice sustain those who want to see the fall of capitalism and the rise of morally liberatory communities, who want these mamas in the eastern DRC to be free and Palestine to be free and Native folks in North America to be free. I have a few notes, a few stories, that may be a bit of a guide toward liberation. That is all I can offer.

I want us to win. I want radical love to win. I want mamas to win.

I want us to love and thrive and recreate the world in the image of joy and laughter. I want our humanity to survive into the next century. On this planet. With these plants and these songs and these myths and dreams and hopes and stories and skills. I want us to be whole and intact, with our ancient traditions of healing and celebrating and mourning. And the only way we are going to be able to do this is to take care of each other.

I am impatient. Our lives are too precious to be sacrificed to the machine of anti-Blackness, anti-Indigeneity, and anti-mothering.

So here is my story about the mamahood. There are of course some tears, but lots of laughter, quirky friends, babies, revolutionaries, singing and dancing, drinking, smoking, anger, revival and survival, large and small families, black-and-white taxis and motorbikes, megacities, and quiet jungles.

This is how we survived. This is what I learned about revolutionary love.

Searching for Paradise

The metal car stopped. I was stuck between the car door on my right and the petite nun on my left. I leaned against the door to open it. My skin sticky and dusty from heat. One deep breath and I stepped into the afternoon light.

Autumn 2003. Already I had been in the West Bank, in Palestine for a week with a "peacemaking" organization when we arrived at Layla's house. In the past few days, the delegation I was with had talked with human rights workers and organizations in Jerusalem. We journeyed through barbed-wire-encased checkpoints staffed by Israeli teenage boys and girls outfitted in military gear and reached our destination, the small Palestinian town in the Bethlehem district, Beit Ummar. Next to this town was the military-guarded Israeli settlement, Efrata.

Layla, our host, wore a long black dress embroidered in traditional Palestinian patterns. A lit cigarette dangled in her right hand as she introduced us to her husband and their three children, two sons and a daughter, Yara, nineteen years old, who was the eldest of the three. The delegation sat on worn couches in the living room in front of bowls overflowing with grapes, sipped tiny glasses of steaming tea with mint leaves floating on top.

Before visiting Beit Ummar, that morning the delegation visited the demolition site of a Palestinian apartment building. We climbed rubble concrete. Random belongings tumbled out of the building as it collapsed. A few Palestinians wandered through the wreckage collecting what remained of their lives: a singed schoolbook, the photograph of an old man, a red sock.

Several Palestinians approached to tell us fragments of their stories. Some of them spoke to us in English. North American human rights workers, who lived in the West Bank and understood some Arabic, interpreted other Palestinians' stories for the delegation. The Israeli military had given only a ten-minute warning that night before shelling and bulldozing the newly built apartment building, killing a Palestinian boy. The military claimed that in the building two young men were hiding who had been accomplices to a suicide bombing a couple of weeks before. A mother pulled me toward her tent. She said her son was too traumatized to go to school. My eyes blurred looking at that small tent on top of broken concrete slabs.

The military had also threatened to demolish Layla's house. But the order had never been executed thanks to Layla's and others' resistance. They had invited human rights workers to sleep in their house night after night during the more intense periods of threat. She fought soldiers. She refused to leave. So far, the house still stood.

I shaded the sun out of my face. "Why do they want to demolish it?"

We followed her outside and she showed us how the Efrata settlement butted against her family's land. "They say we don't have the right papers to prove that we own it."

I had learned in the past few days that this was a common tactic against Palestinian landowners. Because many Palestinians had owned their land for generations and had first acquired the land during the Ottoman Empire, they did not have official documentation proving ownership. Israel used this as a pretext to confiscate families' land and build Israeli settlements on it.

We walked the perimeter of her house and I asked her about the ripening plants. Bushes of white strawberries, pale green cucumbers, pungent red flowers swinging on thin branches and vines. In the garden, she told us that a couple of decades ago Efrata and Beit Ummar had done business and trade with each other. But as the years had passed, and new generations came to power, that relationships had grown cold. The Israeli military became more violent toward the Palestinians. In retaliation, town boys threw rocks at the settlers. The military answered with bullets and housing demolitions.

For dinner she served makluba, a mix of chicken, rice, and vegetables. I scooped up the rice and vegetables onto my plate. After a few minutes she gasped at my plate. "You must eat the chicken." She grabbed the metal tongs.

"Oh. No thank you. I'm not that hungry and I don't really eat a lot of meat."

With tongs punctuating her sentences, she described how the Israeli military had built a fence across their land, dividing the house and garden from the chicken coops. She raised the chickens herself and often had to argue with Israeli soldiers for them to open the gate. Some days she stood for minutes or even hours in the sun waiting to feed her chickens, while the soldiers pointed their guns and laughed.

I ate the piece of chicken.

After dinner we, Layla's family and the international visitors, watched the news in the living room and chatted. Quirky, morbid stories that war survivors tell each other. A soldier who had taken a Palestinian to court for "being armed with a baby." The conservative Muslim families where the boy children treated their sisters like slaves but couldn't boil their own water.

"Yes," Layla said, "you must say to boys the same as you say to girls."

"Oh," replied one of the internationals, "but it is very different here. Yara is the boss of her brothers. She is strong like you."

Folks went to bed one by one, until it was just Yara and I sitting at the dining room table, conversing about the BBC news and writing down the words that the other didn't understand. She wrapped my head in a scarf, Palestinian style, and clucked about my dreadlocks making it difficult for the scarf to lie flat. I showed her how Black girls in the States wrapped scarves around our heads, Nation of Islam style. We talked about the legacy of Malcolm X, the importance of resisting uniformed men's and women's violations, and our shared dislike of most world leaders, especially the current U.S. ones.

In the wee hours of the morning, we retired. I tossed and turned on a thin mattress. The back of my throat felt like sand. A rooster outside of our window crowed.

The next morning, the delegation drank instant coffee and milled about the garden waiting for our taxi van.

Yara came running up to me. "Mai'a, this is for you." She handed me a bright yellow scarf.

Layla said, "That is the scarf her uncle brought her from Syria."

I stumbled out a series of thank yous as the taxi van arrived.

Six months later I returned to the West Bank as a full-time volunteer for the same peacemaking organization, documenting and accompanying Palestinian villages under the threat of violence. Shortly after I landed, the Israeli military demolished a house in Beit Ummar. A couple of us volunteers went to talk to the surviving family.

It was March, the rainy season, and the taxi had almost slipped off the road. We walked to a neighboring house of the recently demolished home. Dressed in layers of plaid shirts and a thin coat, a Palestinian man recounted how he, his wife, and his four children had lost nearly everything they owned. I shivered in the falling mist and tried to take notes but the pages of my notebook were damp and my pen ran out of ink.

After the interview we went to Layla's house for hot coffee and a place to sleep. She gave me a giant hug and whisked me into the house. Layla, with a cigarette between her fingers like a scepter, ordered her sons to bring coffee glasses, each clattering on a miniature saucer.

A few weeks ago, Layla said, the soldiers had invaded Palestinian houses along the edge of Efrata and arrested a couple of young men, one of whom was the son of her husband's first wife. Their household was "upstairs" the hill from Layla's home.

As Layla told the story, miming the soldiers' guns and accents, Yara rolled her eyes. "Mother, your English is horrible. You don't say 'upstairs the hill' you say 'up the hill.'"

Layla pointed to the wall opposite her. Hanging there was a photograph of an old man surrounded by wreaths of synthetic roses doused in glitter. She told us her husband's imprisoned son had made it for the family during his incarceration.

She talked about Yara attending college and majoring in English. Yara cut in: what was needed in Palestine was an Islamic revolution. The Quran was the practical guide for how to lead a spiritual and moral life. One of her brothers interrupted her with a question and she brushed him aside and continued talking. Women were meant to be pregnant as teenagers and in the early twenties, that is when they were most fertile and their bodies were most equipped to carry children.

I looked at the blood-red prison flowers and fingered the bandanna on my head. "Layla? May I have one of your cigarettes?" I felt light-headed by the conversation.

"Of course." She clapped her hands. "I didn't know that you smoked. Yara hates that I smoke. She is always telling me I have to stop . . . She doesn't like that I am Israeli. And she is half-Israeli. She always says: I am not Israeli. I am Muslim." Layla adjusted the scarf pin under her neck.

After the last call to prayer, she and I sat outside exhaling cigarettes, encouraging the smoke to chase the mosquitoes away. She rocked the chair. "Let me tell you about my first husband," she said.

Her family members were Jewish Kurds from Northern Iraq. They had fled to Israel in the middle of the 20th century and had raised her in Jerusalem. She married an Israeli man and gave birth to a son. Her husband had beaten her throughout their marriage until she finally escaped him, but her parents sided with her husband and demanded that she return to him. She refused, but according to law, her husband was the only legitimate custodian of her son. Forced to leave her toddler with him, for more than fifteen years, she had not been allowed to see or speak to her little boy.

Shortly after her escape, she fell in love with a Palestinian man, married him, and became his second wife. She and her children had Israeli citizenship, which allowed them to visit the Israeli prisons and take care of her husband's son, even though neither his Palestinian mother nor father, because they had West Bank identification cards, could visit their son.

Layla and the first wife had become good friends, their daughters only months apart in age. Her first life had been so heavy. But in this life, even though they had to fight to survive, she was happy. A couple of weeks ago she had talked to her first son for the first time since she had left her Israeli husband. He was an adult now.

We sat outside. I brushed mosquitoes from my ears, she brushed smoke from her eyes, and we watched the high crescent moon arc across the night.

Waking up early, I watched Layla's children prepare for school. My stomach clenched. Yara and her mother spoke softly in the next room, then Layla sat on the couch handing me a cigarette. My throat felt raw. I sipped a bit of the coffee dregs. She nodded toward Yara. "She needs money for the taxi to go to school." I gave her seven shekels. "That's all I have."

Yara, dressed in a white shirt, navy blue skirt, and matching scarf, stopped for a moment in the living room, said goodbye, and ducked out of the house. I left for Hebron soon after.

In late September 2004, I woke up, glanced at the clock, jumped out of bed, and stumbled downstairs to the office in the Hebron Old City. Opening the office door, my roommate, an early riser, greeted me. "Did you hear what happened?" My scarf slid off my shaved head as I shook it. Israeli settlers had beaten our two colleagues in at-Tuwani village. Medics were transporting them to an Israeli hospital. Fuck.

The phone rang. It was Hafez.

"Hafez! It's Mai'a."

"Mai'a! How are you?"

"Good. Alhamdulillah."

I had been living in the West Bank for half a year with a human rights group and had spent a week living in Hafez's home in at-Tuwani village. Hafez, with sandy-colored skin and an easy smile, was the only person in the village who spoke English and had seemed amused by this Black American woman with a shaved head who asked a million questions in halting Arabic.

Seconds after I hung up the phone, it rang again; journalists and human rights workers had caught wind of the attack.

Cal, my best friend and coworker from the United States, and I hired taxis to the Palestinian village as our colleagues lay in an Israeli hospital.

I sat with Hafez, smiling and serious, in at-Tuwani and drank sweet sage tea, listening to the story of the attacks. He pointed to the Havat Ma'on, an outpost that shelters Israeli settler fanatics. My colleagues had come to at-Tuwani village to walk with children from the neighboring village, Tuba, to the nearest elementary school in at-Tuwani. Their first day was a quiet journey. On their second day with the Tuba children, Israelis from the Ma'on outpost, with masks and baseball bats, had surprise-attacked. The children ran to Tuba with only a few scratches. The Israeli gang targeted the internationals. One colleague suffered a pierced lung and broken rib, the other, a broken arm and knee.

That night I lay in what the villagers referred to in English as "the museum," unable to fall asleep. It was a large stone room, modeled after the caves that dotted the hills, cool to the touch in the summer and warm in the winter. Stones had been mortared originally with animal feces between three hundred and five hundred years ago. Women throughout the Hebron hills sewed and wove in the evening, improvising their needlework patterns. They contributed their cross-stitch and weaving to the museum in hope that internationals who visited at-Tuwani would buy their wares. Our neighbor up the hill had inherited the museum from her father and ran it while mothering three sons, running a household, and organizing meetings for half a dozen villages.

The last time I had been in the museum, the afternoon heat stuck to my neck. An Italian woman and I were laughing with some of the village girls and women in the museum. Behind us an older woman wove a belt on a small handmade loom, a long floppy needle darting between the warp and weft. I smiled at two of the girls who worked in the village store and asked about the different crafts displayed. I pointed to red and orange wall hangings, which, it turned out, kept fresh bread warm. And the small conical item with metal bells and beads? They giggled. They called the Italian woman over to them. The women placed it on her head wrapping the beads through her wavy hair. It was the traditional headdress for the wedding. What a beautiful bride!

Naim's teenage daughters worked in the only business other than the museum in at-Tuwani, a small corner store. It consisted of one room, with a freezer under the window that held cold water, juice, and soda. The shelves held canned foods, batteries, candies, and assorted house goods. Next to the freezer they had stacked crates filled with fresh tomatoes, cauliflower, and limes. The girls greeted customers, answered questions, gossiped, and counted money and stock, their head-scarves sometimes slipping a bit off their hair.

That evening, we sat on a roof brimming with half of the village, a couple of my colleagues, and me. The television flickered. The two girls from the store squeezed red mud out of a tiny hole pricked in a plastic sandwich bag onto my colleague's hand. A couple of older women asked me if I too wanted to be decorated. I shrugged and said yes, if they wanted to. They called to the sisters. The television played a movie about thieves and lovers while they turned my palm toward the stars and asked for the name of the boy with whom I was in love. The girls inscribed the letter 'K,' for Cal, my boyfriend, in henna on my palm. They decorated the rest of my hand with curlicues and dots. We stumbled over the pebbles in the path on our way to our sleeping bags. Before I went to bed I washed the mud off with bottled water. The next morning my hands, streaked red, looked more like they were recovering from the pox rather than promising me to my beloved.

A couple of weeks later, as my comrades lay in an Israeli hospital, I slept restlessly. It was my first night back in the village. I dreamed of dyed yarns, bruised torsos, cream-colored dresses with maroon designs, black dresses shining with gold thread, snarling men transforming into fairy tale trolls, navy blue and green bags with tiny Palestinian flags sewn on the flap, baseball bats crushing bones, beaded jewelry, and woven marriage veils hanging on the stone walls.

That night the father of the Tuba children had told us that his children were willing to walk the short path to school if we, internationals, walked with them. The next morning, I washed my face and drank a couple of sips of treated water, and then we walked to Tuba. For a moment, we stopped on the edge of the desert and just looked at the Ma'on settlement and forest. Then, we darted through the hills and arrived at a black wooden door of a cave, their home. The mother served us bread, honey, butter, and tea. The children hid in the shadows next to the light coming from the cracked door. Then we, children and internationals, wound around the hills, creeping passed the Ma'on barns, forest, and settlement and sprinted toward the at-Tuwani elementary school. My body was a machine; I couldn't afford to feel.

Hafez stood behind his house, hands on his hips, smoking a cigarette, and asked how the walk had been. Mish mushkile. No problem. He served us tiny glasses that rattled on a silver-colored tray. We sat in front of his house chain-smoking and sipping mint tea.

While the children recited their homework in class that day, an Israeli military Hummer crept over the dirt roads and stopped next to my colleague and me. The soldier adjusted his reflective sunglasses. "You should not walk beside the settlement to Tuba anymore. We cannot guarantee your safety."

"The children have a right to go to school. Expecting them to walk up to ten kilometers through the mountains to go to school is just mean. They are kids; they can't hurt anybody." He shrugged, repeated his warning, and drove away. I could barely pass air through my lungs. We walked back to the village store, shaking, and told Hafez.

"We see that even the soldiers are scared of the settlers," he said. "And the soldiers are from here."

"From where?" I asked.

"From the settlements, here."

At-Tuwani is a thousand-year-old village, with 150 to 200 people. Around 1980, the Jewish National Fund planted a forest nature preserve at the edge of at-Tuwani. The government promised that everyone, Israeli and Palestinian, would have access to the forest. In 1981, an Israeli military brigade founded the Ma'on settlement next to the forest preserve. At first, the settlement was just tents and caravans. Then, the settlers built houses and brought running water and electricity. Dov Dribben, a twenty-eight-year-old American-Israeli, along with other Israeli settlers, moved into the forest, named it Havat Ma'on, and sowed vineyards, olive groves, and fruit trees. They proclaimed that they were fulfilling God's will and redeeming Israel. Dribben began to build a stone house for him and his family. After several confrontations between Palestinians and Dribben, a Palestinian wrested Dribben's gun from his hands during an altercation and shot him. In protest to the shooting, hundreds of Israeli settlers reoccupied the forest. Dribben's unfinished house became a symbolic center of the Israeli protesters. Four days after Dribben's death, under the orders of Ehud Barak, the Israeli prime minister, one thousand Israeli soldiers, and police evicted twenty Palestinian families, totaling around four hundred people, from their ancient homes neighboring Havat Ma'on and evacuated Israelis from Havat Ma'on itself. Outlaw Israeli settlers returned to Havat Ma'on, and occupied trailers, tents, and abandoned school buses in the forest; Israeli military patrolled the area every couple of hours, protecting these settlers.

The settlers remaining in the forest attacked children walking to school and now, the internationals accompanying them. They poisoned at-Tuwani's drinking well with dead chickens. They conjured military mandates that ordered the destruction of olive groves and family crops.

That evening Hafez knelt in the museum with us, sipping tea and discussing our strategy for the next day. The soldier had clearly told us that the military had given the settlers a blank check to do what they wanted. Could we do this for another day and survive? After hours of talking, crying, panicking, and whispering, we came to the conclusion the only thing that we could do was put one foot in front of another and walk past the settlements.

We couldn't sleep that night. For hours, we sang protest songs, hymns, gospel songs, love songs, and bawdy songs about thieves and lovers. Finally, the international men went outside to sleep and we women curled into our sleeping bags inside the museum and burned coiled incense to scare away the mosquitoes.

Thursday morning, an Israeli and German couple came to walk with us. The children and their father were waiting for us at the edge of the Tuba. The mountains shaded us from the sunrise dusting the sky. I kept smoking cigarettes, feeling my heart would kick my ribcage, so I knew I was still alive. We kept an eye on the settlement, a series of single-family homes with triangle roofs, looking out of place in the Palestinian mountains, more like what I would find in an American suburb than in the West Bank. As we approached the settlement, an encampment of soldiers and trucks blocked the path. The international boys approached the soldiers, while we women sat with the children. They argued loudly. The children stared at the soldiers and settlements, refusing to blink. We, one Italian, one German, and one African-American woman, started to sing. "Yesterday" by the Beatles, "Marching in the Light of God" in four languages, "Oh Freedom," and "Father Abraham."

> *Father Abraham had many sons*
> *Many sons had Father Abraham*
> *I am one of them*
> *And so are you*
> *So, let's just praise the Lord!*

We made up words when we couldn't remember them. We acted out the songs. And then we started to dance. We shot jazz hands in the air and hummed Broadway songs. The children stared like we were crazy. They sat on slabs of rock, clutching their backpacks in their laps. The eldest girl gave me a sly smile. We belted out John Lennon's "Imagine" as if it was closing time at the local bar and we didn't want to go home.

The international men returned to tell us that the Israeli military had declared the path next to the settlement a closed military zone. No one but settlers could walk on it. Fuck. The men went back to the soldiers and negotiated, while calling every lawyer we knew in Israel.

The soldiers compromised. The children could go to at-Tuwani, but not us, and they would escort the children to school.

Hours passed. We were stuck. We ran out of water and kicked stones. We did not know another path to Tuwani; we had no compass, no map. The minutes slowed. The Israeli guy called in to a radio station, clutching the phone and grinning. We were marooned in the desert, such a dramatic opening for his radio interview. After his interview, we talked in circles. Exhausted, one by one, we lay down in the sand to rest. I shook my head and dusted off my clothes. "We have to get up," I said. "We can't just sleep. It will cause sunstroke."

The Israeli guy sauntered to the settlement "to check it out." He returned a few minutes later, smirking because the settlement manager had offered him a bottle of water. But of course he refused to take a gift from a settler. I stuck out my chest, put my hands on my hips, and lowered my voice. We were collapsing in the desert from dehydration. His German girlfriend's wrists looked like they would snap if she breathed too hard. "We need water." He shuffled back to the settlement and returned with a green plastic two-liter bottle of water and the news that the manager of the settlement would let us walk through the Ma'on settlement to the highway. From there, we could walk to at-Tuwani. We staggered to the tar highway in the high noon, drinking water and laughing. We had escaped.

The next day was Friday, no school. Israeli activists arrived like a swarm of bees, with a large white banner that they unfurled onto the dirt to finish the lettering. They paraded an impromptu demonstration on the Tuba/at-Tuwani path to the settlement. I lingered next to Hafez, both of us with burning cigarettes hanging on our fingers. The protesters chanted in Hebrew, as they moved toward the edge of the settlement. They met the Israeli soldiers who reiterated that the path was under a military closure.

Most of the protesters, in ripped shirts, pants with political patches, overgrown matted hair, and faded backpacks, wandered around the path. Then the Israeli activist leader announced that they were going to the forest to confront the settlers. I looked at Hafez and his brother-in-law Nasser. "Do you think that's a good idea?" I asked. The Israelis had not sought permission of anyone who lived in at-Tuwani.

I tapped the shoulder of a tall, messy-haired Israeli who spoke English and Arabic fluently. He nodded and got the attention of the protest leader. I explained my critiques. Israeli settlers had beaten Palestinians and internationals. The Israeli military reiterated daily that the settlers were going to hurt us again, but we had promised to walk the children to school no matter what the military or settlers threatened. The Israeli activists would leave that afternoon and return to their homes, but the goal of those who lived in the village was to ensure that the Tuba children could walk to school using the shortest path there. How was pissing off a bunch of crazy settlers going to accomplish this? He cocked his head, waved his hand, blinked twice, and replied, "I don't understand your English."

Hafez and Nasser said the risk was too great for them and turned to the village. I walked behind the Israelis, chanting, on the dirt path circling the forest. A settler boy, no more than seven years old, with a camera, stood in front of his mother. She, dressed in loose-fitting off-white cotton clothes, yelled at us in Hebrew: Arab-lover, coward, Nazi. The father sported cherry tomato-red hair topped with an indigo kippah. He held a rifle against his shoulder. They looked like aggro versions of Mother Earth hippies. Plastic tarps were tied to tree trunks. Underneath the tarps, a metal pot and cup lay upturned on a dirty blanket.

I imagined what I looked like to them at that moment, dingy clothes, cracked lips, and ashy skin.

The Israelis' parade returned to Tel Aviv. The museum was just as we had left it that morning: dark and mute. Sheep brayed in the distance.

The next day I had a terrible headache and my bones ached. One of my colleagues had a fever. We lay on our sleeping bags in the Museum. Outside the village men were building us a little shack and outhouse, our new home. Cal, my boyfriend, grew weak and fell unconscious in our brand-new outhouse, crashing his head into the corrugated tin that stood in place of a door and then he flopped like a dehydrated fish onto the sand.

Life over the next days blurred into sunrises, stars, sand, burnt hills, scraggy flowers, sheep feces dotting the mountain paths and canyons, and bittersweet coffee; it blurred into the smell of gas stoves, fresh bread, mosquito repellant, cheap Israeli and Palestinian cigarettes, treated water, unwashed sleeping bags, and Israeli soldiers yelling rough orders from Hummer trucks, orders they themselves seemed not to understand. Nearly all of us fell sick from flu, diarrhea, and dehydration, dizzy from surviving another day and then another day after that.

And yet in some ways I still felt safer in the village than I did in Hebron city. The Israelis were threatening to kill us, but unlike in Hebron, the Palestinians in at-Tuwani were respectful for the most part. I could walk around the village without dealing with the intense street harassment that characterized my time in the city. No lewd comments, no racist jokes, no Palestinian boys throwing rocks at me or stalking me on the sidewalks.

We moved into the little concrete building with a corrugated tin roof, our shack next to the museum. I woke up with flea bites on my arms and legs. One morning, after we had walked the children to school, Hafez showed us how to clean the floor, air our mattresses, cook on a single gas burner stove (even though he usually declined to eat the dinners we had prepared), store food, make tea, gather water from the well, and clean our outhouse.

Journalists, documentarians, human rights workers, lawyers, and war tourists visited the village. I gave tours and introduced them to Saber, the village "mayor," weathered with fierce eyes. In the Museum he told at-Tuwani's long history while visitors admired and purchased crafts and jewelry. Village leaders were excited about the publicity and the ways that the world's focus on the village could open up the possibility that they would survive the daily crush of Israeli violence. More specifically, they hoped the attention would pressure the Israeli government and military to protect the children walking to school.

I had talked on the phone with the U.S. consulate a couple of times after the attack on our colleagues. Two consulate representatives arrived in a shiny SUV with dark tinted windows. That morning they had called and requested the exact address where we would be meeting. I giggled; as if the village had street signs and house numbers!

Saber, the "mayor," wizened and stoic, carried a plastic expandable folder choked with documents. Village men followed. The lady from the Consulate only had permission to travel a one-hundred-meter radius from the Museum and had to leave after two hours. We sat down, drank tea, while Saber told the history of these small Palestinian villages and the Israeli settlements' arrival in the southern Hebron hills. His well-organized papers detailed every official Israeli military closure and governmental order to demolish a Palestinian house, mosque, and barn. Every building, he said, including the school and the museum, was illegal according to the Israeli government. The settlements gobbled more land to serve their burgeoning population and ambitions, but allowed no Palestinian to build, not even the outhouse and shed the at-Tuwani folk had built for us internationals. Israelis had beaten, bullied, and threatened the villagers, poisoned the village wells, killed their livestock, stole land, and traumatized children and grandparents. The representative's eyes widened. The other men nodded their heads, murmuring. Too soon she climbed into the black truck with air-conditioning and leather seats and rode back to Israel on highway roads on which the

Israeli government allowed no Palestinian to walk, much less drive. She left copies of *Time* and *Newsweek* and explained that even though I was a U.S. citizen, the consulate could offer me no protection because it had warned all U.S. citizens not to enter the Occupied Territories.

Before I went to Palestine, as the media bombarded me with images of veiled Muslim women, young women suicide bombers, stone-throwers, and the fear of Islam, I listened daily to "First Writing Since," a poetic response to September 11th, by Suheir Hammad, an African-American/Palestinian woman. "The only people who know what we are feeling right now/ Live in the West Bank and the Gaza Strip."

I was twenty-three years old. For the past couple of years, I had been a performance poet and ran a small media organization, a community theatre, and an art gallery in Appalachian Virginia.

That late winter, in 2003, we had protested against Bush's invasion of Iraq. The largest global protests in the history of humankind and it hadn't mattered, Bush and his "coalition of the willing" bombed Iraq into chaos.

When I was a kid, I'd watch the news with my father. He explained geopolitics as a series of games of power that nations and leaders played against each other. "It's like a chess game."

In the *Washington Post*, I read about the Middle East. I pulled out the atlas and moved my fingers against the rough paper, tracing alliances and enemies. Iraq, Gaza, Israel, Lebanon, Ramallah, Kurds, Shi'a, Fatah, Arafat, Sunni, Sinai. I heard a deep whisper from my belly, "You should just go there." My hand trembled. I flipped through the pages. Jordan, Egypt, Saudi Arabia. Al-Qaeda and Hamas. Ariel Sharon, Judea and Samaria, separation walls and settlements. "There is freedom and courage there," the whisper promised.

Yeah, I should just go to where the U.S. empire put so much of its resources, its military, its scapegoats. Protesting in the United States didn't make a difference, but Western human rights activists in Baghdad and Palestine were resisting U.S. imperialism, putting themselves directly in the path of U.S.-funded bombs and soldiers.

Palestinians were defending their homeland from the U.S.-financed Israeli military and demanding a revolution. What did that kind of intense resistance against colonialism look like up close? Did it feel like freedom?

Would Palestinians defeating the U.S. empire and Israeli colonialism make us all more free?

Che Guevara had said that U.S. Americans' work was to defeat the U.S. empire in the belly of the beast. But Palestine, Iraq, and Afghanistan were the imperial "hot spots" where maybe we who believed in freedom had a chance of winning.

My family was not happy about my decision to join a ten-day delegation to the Israeli/Palestinian conflict zone. They were definitely not happy about my decision to move to the West Bank for the foreseeable future.

My mother pressed her lips tight and refused to talk about or acknowledge it.

My father stayed with my mother for a few months in her DC suburban house that autumn of 2003. He stretched out his lanky, tall body on Mom's couch, watching CNN.

"You see that? See that?" He pointed to the large clouds of gray smoke and uniformed men with rifles filling the television screen. "This is where you want to go?"

I turned toward the TV. "Palestine is more than just what you see on the television."

He growled, "That conflict has nothing to do with you."

"Well, I guess it does now since I'm going to be living there."

He waved his hand, "And these Palestinians don't care about you."

Images of Layla and Yara flitted through my mind. A yellow scarf. Seeded grapes. Being taught to wrap hijab around my hair.

My father and I had had this argument for years. He had been a Black radical activist in the 1960s in Southern California, organizing with the Black Panthers, and felt a deep betrayal by Black radical activists. He never told me the details of what happened but had made it clear he wanted me to "Stay far away from all that mess. They didn't care about me. They don't give a damn about you."

But he'd insisted in my teenage years that I read books like *The Autobiography of Malcolm X* and *They Came Before Columbus*, collections of Black poets and college surveys of African-American history; that I articulate where I stood on pan-Africanism, third-world internationalism, Garvey and du Bois, the racist witch hunts against Billie Holiday and Nina Simone. From them, I came to believe in revolution the way other people believe in Jesus. And in Palestine I saw a people using Black radical organizing tools to demand their own liberation, to demand a revolution, a contemporary ancient vision of paradise.

"Dad, I'm not doing this because Palestinians care about me. Palestinians don't know me. I'm going because I care about freedom and self-determination."

I looked at the TV again. A small woman was walking over a sand hill with a baby tied to her front and a plastic basket on her head. Maybe Palestine was a hellish war zone, maybe it was a paradise. The land of milk and honey. Zion. A place that inspired poems.

The West Bank desert villages in many ways reminded me of rural South Carolina where my mother's Black and Indigenous family were from. Even though I had grown up in the Washington, DC, metro area, I had spent the summers and holidays on my family's land with my grandparents and cousins. Among the pine trees and slow, simple days was where I had first learned to write poems about hope and struggle and stars.

Those sandy roads. Simple houses built out of wood and concrete and metal roofs. The slow, proud drawl. The ways that religious speech peppered the conversation. "Praise god. God is god. Pray for her, she is struggling."

Men and women who spent their days out in the fields. Dinner plucked from the garden. Food and drink offered always when a guest entered your home. Women sitting together in the dusk, drinking tea, shelling peas and telling stories, the air buzzing with flies and mosquitos, while the children played underfoot and in the sparse grasses outside. Scarves tied to women's heads, simple shift dresses and plastic house shoes. Oven-hot summers and wet winters.

Your second cousin was also your best friend; your aunt was also your neighbor and your schoolteacher. Close-knit communities had learned that sticking together was the only way to survive a world that wanted you destroyed. My family had protected our acres of land during Jim Crow against the KKK and white supremacists who resented our small moments of freedom and comfort.

Palestinians were putting their lives on the line for their people's freedom, for the chance to create a paradise for their children and their ancestors. They had asked for internationals to come and witness and share in their struggle against Israeli occupation. And some small voice inside of me said, "Yes, I understand you, like me, are searching for paradise against the forces that want to destroy your land."

A year later, in early September, the Israeli military came to the at-Tuwani olive groves and uprooted over forty trees. I hiked a mile along the highway and checked the batteries in my camera. Branches and roots littered the ground. An elderly petite woman came towards me screaming. She cried out, "Look at what the military did to my land!" I asked the village spokesmen what had happened to the trees. They each quoted her, translating her grief. She was Hafez's mother. Less than a year ago, she, a mother and grandmother, had been beaten by the Israeli settlers.

After living there for a week, I staggered into the Old City Hebron office, with the flu. I slept past morning meeting and remained in bed all day. I watched the sunlight pour through the curtains. A day later, I was in front of the computer, coughing and typing an email. The office phone rang. Settlers had attacked the internationals in the southern Hebron hills again, but this time they had managed to take photographs of the masked settlers. I reached in my pocket for a cigarette, walked outside with Cal, and struck a match.

That evening when I arrived in at-Tuwani, Layla called me. She had heard through the grapevine where I was. "My daughter, Mai'a, please be safe. The settlers do crazy things. I love you. Come and visit us in Beit Ummar. We will have olives soon."

One More for the Revolution

I pushed the thin bedsheet off onto the floor and lay still listening to children playing in the Bethlehem side streets. The heat in the house rose and my stomach felt nauseated, like I was coming down with the flu.

I rolled over and counted the weeks since my last period.

Cal and I were married in the summer of 2005 at his parents' cabin in the Upper Peninsula of Michigan. We drank whisky on fishing boats and camped outside with our friends. According to most of our friends, we were an odd match. He was six feet tall and white, grew up in a small conservative town, spoke minimally, wore all-black everything, and listened to Suicidal Tendencies on full blast. I was the Black radical poet from the DMV who loved painting in the afternoons and dancing to hip hop until sunrise. I met him at a month-long nonviolent direct-action training in Chicago in the winter of 2003. We talked about books and smoked cigarettes in the dirty snow. In the West Bank, when he had asked me to marry him in December 2004, I said yes without hesitation.

We moved back to the West Bank in the spring of 2006. And after two months, he had flown back to the U.S. to officiate his best friend's wedding. He'd be gone for two weeks, while I stayed behind.

I walked into the kitchen, drank a glass of water, contemplating my options. I picked up my Nokia mobile phone and called Hawwa, a Palestinian woman who lived in the Bethlehem district.

"Hey, Hawwa . . . I have a question . . . Where do I buy a pregnancy test?"

"What? Do you think you are . . . ?"

"Well, my period is late and I've been feeling sick."

"Oh my god. I am so sorry. What are you going to do? Most women go to the doctor's office and have a blood test. It's the most accurate."

"Okay, but I just want to pee on a stick in my own bathroom." I didn't know any doctors in Palestine whom I could trust and I didn't want to be an unaccompanied young Black woman going to a strange doctor and announce that I might be pregnant and my husband was out of the country. Bethlehem was a small town.

"Well I don't think there is a pharmacy in Bethlehem where you can buy it." She said, "Maybe in Ramallah . . . ? I remember seeing them once when I was in a pharmacy in Ramallah."

Ramallah was the de facto capital city of the West Bank. It was about twenty miles from Bethlehem, but it could take two and half hours to travel in cramped taxis between the two cities, because of Israeli checkpoints and roadblocks.

Then, from the background, Hawwa's husband, Andrew, suggested in his Welsh accent that I go to a pharmacy in West Jerusalem.

I sighed. West Jerusalem was closer, but it still meant I'd have to endure one of the biggest and most militarized checkpoints just to leave the Bethlehem area.

From the outside, the Bethlehem checkpoint looked like a large bus station or a small airport. Inside, it was lines of people being herded through one or two caged stalls. Their bags, purses, and boxes gliding on conveyor belts and passing through metal detectors. Israeli soldiers, guns hanging on their shoulders, demanded IDs and permits. Sometimes the checkpoint took ten minutes, other times it was hours. But at least it was closer than Ramallah.

I called Hannah, a U.S. American who lived in the Bethlehem area, and they told me they were already planning to go to West Jerusalem that very afternoon. They were a redhead from Oregon and worked in one of the local Palestinian NGOs.

I could tag along with them and buy a pregnancy test in West Jerusalem.

What if I was a mother? What if I was a mother in Palestine?

When Hannah and I arrived in Jerusalem, we went to the Jewish quarter of the Old City and entered the first pharmacy we saw. Rows of pink boxes of pregnancy tests behind the cashier's head. I bought one, wrapped it in a scarf and stuffed it into my backpack like it was a fragile vase or a bomb.

Then we went to meet Sasha, tall with short dark hair, in an NGO office in West Jerusalem, and the three of us walked to a house party thrown by Israeli anarchists. One woman, with matted light-brown hair, was in the kitchen making stuffed grape leaves, following a recipe in a book of traditional dishes. The book was propped up next to the stove. She undercooked the rice and fumbled some grains into the stiff grape leaves.

"Do you want some help?" I offered after a while.

"Oh," she said, "this is a traditional Israeli dish."

"Well, I used to live with, like, a couple of Palestinian women who'd make it all the time and so they taught me to . . ."

She turned her back to me and continued fumbling with the leaves.

Later the party guests gathered around a long, low table and ate the dinner. The undercooked rice sagged out of the leaves. I swallowed a couple of mouthfuls and washed it down with cheap, sweet red wine.

Shefa and her daughter, thirty-year-old Kefa, the Palestinian women I lived with two years previously, would have mocked me if I had made warak dawali like this or if I had called it "a traditional Israeli dish."

The first time I had learned how to make it was in the spring of 2004. Shefa had sent me to Jerusalem to purchase grape leaves so that she could make it for my friends and colleagues in Hebron. She gave me directions in the Old City to the street seller who had the best leaves. When I returned, she shook her head—I had gotten the wrong ones. These leaves were too old, too thick, they would be no good for the dish. The next day she sent me back to the Old City. I found the correct seller, his vegetables spread on a blanket on the cobblestones. I handed him Shefa's handwritten note and a few shekels in exchange for a small plastic bag of grape leaves.

The next morning, after the morning house cleaning was done, Shefa, Kefa, and I sat on a faded blanket with a pot of freshly cooked rice and beef and a pile of soaked grape leaves. They taught me to put the rice on the leaf and to roll the grape leaves tightly between my fingers. Some leaves you had to discard because they were too weak to hold the rice. Shefa smiled, "Kwayyes, Mai'a, kwayyes ktiir." I nodded at the encouragement. "It's getting easier. It's kind of like rolling a cigarette." She laughed.

They lived in a small house next to the Tomb of Lazarus, in the town of al-Azariya, just two miles from Jerusalem. For most of their lives they had basically considered themselves to be Jerusalemites. But that spring, Israel had started building the Apartheid Wall to divide al-Azariya from the rest of East Jerusalem. Shefa and Kefa were no longer allowed to visit their friends and family in Jerusalem without written Israeli permission.

As I drank wine with the Israeli anarchists, I imagined how elated Shefa would be if I visited with news that I was pregnant.

Today was Sasha's birthday, so we left the party and celebrated with cake and brown liquor in a tiny park. We sat in the dark on a small white bench next to a creek and talked about birthdays and babies. Hannah didn't want to have children. They had a genetic blood disease that they didn't want to pass on to children. Sasha said she did not want to become one more breeder. "There are already too many people on the planet. It's irresponsible to, like, have even more people. And like, this world is horrible, how could I bring an innocent child into this world?" But I knew life was miraculous and Black and Brown children were always a blessing. Palestinian mothers were in constant danger, yet they seemed to believe more in the future than they believed in safety.

I turned to Sasha. "I read this article written about Palestinian feminism, and one Palestinian mother said that when she had another child she saw it as 'one more for the revolution.'" I wasn't giving up my life, I was making my life wider.

We took a taxi to the Bethlehem checkpoint and walked inside the large warehouse-like building. It was empty. No one at the gates or in the little booths. No one running the conveyor belt where we put our bags so they could be scanned. No Israeli guards. No Palestinians. Just the sound of the electricity, the whir of the fans, and the crackle of the neon lights. The three of us stood there shocked.

"Hello? Hello? Shalooooom?"

I looked at the ceiling, "Are there cameras . . . or . . . ?"

"Should we just go? I mean . . . are we allowed to just go if there is no one here?"

Finally, we ducked under the turnstile and ran through the open gates and doors until we emerged outside one of the most heavily fortified checkpoints in the West Bank. Deep exhale.

"Wow. Just wow."

"I can't believe that no one stopped us. Shit."

"That was a fucking miracle."

For a moment we just stared at the checkpoint building and at each other in awe. Then we flagged a taxi and returned to our respective homes.

I peed in a disposable cup, stuck the plastic wand into the urine, and messaged with Cal as I waited.

And then, two clear pink lines.

It was midnight in Bethlehem. I was alone in the apartment. Pregnant. Everything felt possible.

Cal and I had found our apartment, a couple of months ago, through my friend Daya, a Palestinian woman I met in 2004 while living in the old city of Hebron. In her early twenties, Daya was the only Hebronite woman I knew who walked the streets without hijab. Instead she wore button-down shirts, dark slacks, and short dark hair framing her pale face. We'd meet in a downtown ice cream shop and groan about being harassed on Hebron streets. Both of us looked like foreigners. Hebron was one of the conservative West Bank cities. Its social life centered the long wedding seasons when young women spent weeks being scrutinized as potential daughters-in-law. "But if you can't date, then how do you know if you two are really compatible?" I asked her as I sipped the after-ice-cream coffee. She shook her head and said, "A lot of the men watch porn instead."

Bethlehem, where she attended university, was different. It had a strong Christian presence, which meant liquor stores along with the sunburned Holy Land tourists and early morning church bells. Bars, dance clubs, and women in short-sleeved shirts and skirts that showed their calves. Single women like Daya could live without chaperones and earn their own money and a bit more social freedom.

A week after we arrived in Palestine, Daya introduced us to her ex-landlord, Rami. He, his wife, and their four children lived on the basement-floor apartment and had a sandwich shop on the ground floor. He showed us the apartment: a small kitchen, living room, bathroom, and bedroom with two twin beds pushed together. Secondhand furniture and kitchenware, a large crack cutting the living room wall. Fruit vines and pomegranate trees in the backyard. It was perfect. We moved in the next day, bought Taybeh beers from downstairs, and sat on the roof to watch the fireworks celebrating a late spring wedding.

Daya invited us to a house party in Beit Sahour, a small town neighboring Bethlehem, a couple of days later. Lights down low. Salsa, hip hop, rock, Arab pop. Cheap liquor and sugary juice in disposable cups. Clouds of cigarette smoke.

Most of the guests were from the United States or Europe, visiting for a couple of months, students, journalists, photographers, trust-fund kids, NGO workers, activists against the apartheid wall. This revolving door of foreigners was anchored by Palestinians who spoke excellent English and were translators, and NGO workers (often paid less than their foreign counterparts), tutors, and English-language students. Italian, Spanish, French, English, and Arabic jumbled together, as people found lovers, housemates, playmates, job opportunities, political debates, travel tips.

"What's your name? Where are you from? Oh . . . what are you doing here? How long have you been here? Oh, you're with what organization? Oh, what do they do? Where are they based? Cool, cool. Yeah, so how were the checkpoints today? How long did you spend? How long are you here for? Right, right." Geopolitics was small talk.

At the party, I met Asim, a radio journalist for a Palestinian-led NGO. He was casually intense, with a stocky build and an easy laugh. We chatted about the weather, mutual acquaintances, and what it meant to be a Beit Sahour Christian living under the new Hamas legislature.

Cal got a job as a copy editor for a Palestinian news agency in Bethlehem, and a week after meeting Asim at the house party, I ended up working for him as an editor, writer, and radio broadcast journalist in Beit Sahour.

In January 2006, Palestinians elected a Hamas-majority legislature. In response the United States, Israel, and other nations imposed economic sanctions on the Palestinian government, claiming that Hamas was a terrorist organization. Many middle-class Palestinians were government workers, teachers, and bureaucrats, and suddenly the government couldn't pay them. The working classes—restaurant workers, taxi drivers, and builders—lost income since folks couldn't afford their services. As the summer came and the heat index rose, I overheard folks' money worries in cafés and the market.

On a weekly, and sometimes daily, basis Israel kidnapped elected parliamentary members in the middle of the night for the "crime" of being members of Hamas. Then, in early June, Israelis killed a Hamas government leader with an airstrike in Gaza. The next day, I sat in my landlord's café watching the evening news. Corpses in the sun on a Gaza sandy beach after Israel bombed the beach. A little girl screamed in terror and grief for minutes, running and collapsing in the sand. An Israeli bombing had just killed seven of her family members at four thirty in the afternoon. The newscaster read out the name of the martyrs.

Two weeks later, Gaza militants retaliated by kidnapping an Israeli soldier and sneaking him back to Gaza via underground tunnels. In response, the Israeli military announced "Operation Summer Rains," in which they bombed and invaded Gaza by air and sea. They destroyed the only electrical plant in Gaza, launched airstrikes against the university, and destroyed families' homes.

Most days I edited news briefs on laptops in a small set of white offices. Then I entered a handmade sound booth, with gray foam on the walls, and read the briefs into a microphone, while Asim sat on the other side of the booth regulating the digital sound controls and producing the daily radio news show.

The briefs I read sounded like, "While Israel attacks Gaza, Hezbollah militants have captured two Israeli soldiers. Hezbollah says they will release the Israeli soldiers only if Israel first releases the Lebanese Hezbollah prisoners. Instead of releasing the Hezbollah prisoners, Israel has continued bombing Gaza and has commenced bombing southern Lebanon as well."

The world around us, in Lebanon, Gaza, and Hebron, unraveled, but at least the beers remained cheap. We spent our evenings smoking cigarettes, discussing the news, and watching the World Cup in Beit Sahour's loud, late-night restaurants or in our colleagues' apartments. The shops sold football memorabilia and Brazil's colors lined the streets. I didn't follow the beautiful game but cheered for the team with the largest amount of dark-skinned folks. Usually they won. In the mornings, after Cal left for work, I brewed Turkish coffee to take the edge off the late nights and read the Arab news blogs. Around 3:00 p.m., I'd take a taxi to the news agency, walk up the stairs, and with Asim and our workmates tackle the crisis of the day.

In those offices, we debated how to describe Israeli aggression to a Western, English-speaking audience. When young men from Gaza retaliated against Israeli aggression, how should we describe it? Were they using homemade rockets? Short-range rockets? Were they symbolic rockets, since, unlike Israeli weapons, Gazan rockets caused little-to-no structural or bodily damage? Were the young men militants? Fighters? Terrorists?

How could our news reporting support the Palestinian people? Should we be openly critical of the Palestinian political parties that claimed to speak and act for the people? Should we lead the daily news with the bloodiest story or focus on stories that represented everyday life in Palestine?

One evening after work, Brian, who was a McGill University student with pale hair and a thin face, Asim, and I ordered beers and olives in a nearby restaurant.

"We have very little Palestinian women in the broadcast. When we focus solely on militant response and Israeli response we act as if Palestinian women only show up in the narrative as victims."

Brian scoffed and ashed his cigarette. "This is serious news. Not some little human-interest story. There's plenty of that shit out there, NGOs showing that Palestinians are peaceful and stuff." He glowered, "This is war."

I sighed. He had been in the West Bank for just a few months. The waiter took empty bottles off the table and asked if we wanted another round.

"Talking about women in the conflict is not just placating those who want to hear 'nonviolent' stories or want to hear how 'bad those Arabs are to their wives.' It's about getting at the heart of the conflict. How do we tell interesting stories that illuminate the conflict? Yes, this is war. No doubt. But, if all we talk about is blood and guns we are letting the Western media control the discourse."

"Well, Mai'a, maybe you know what is going on here, but a lot of people back home don't. And we need to show them as graphically as possible."

A couple of weeks later I joined a friend in the northern West Bank, for an International Solidarity Movement (ISM) action in Bilin. The ISM was a pro-Palestine-solidarity, direct-action organization that brought large numbers of mostly white Westerners and Jews to Palestine to nonviolently oppose the Israeli occupation.

Bilin was a small town outside of Ramallah. At first glance looked like most small Palestinian towns. Sandy paths and sand-colored buildings. Sparse grass and rolling hills. Since the beginning of 2005, the wall split the town in two. Palestinians and internationals protested it every Friday morning for the past year and a half.

On an overcast morning, we marched with a Palestinian couple to the Wall and applauded as they married. A wedding procession of family and friends. Her white dress and veil. His black pants and maroon jacket. A bouquet of roses.

We protested next to a large metal gate. Israeli construction vehicles parked on the other side the fence. On our side, lines of Israeli soldiers armed and in riot gear stood in front of us.

Then, a Palestinian boy threw a rock at the Israeli soldiers and hit a helmet. Soldiers fired tear gas and sound bombs. Anger and surprise roared to life as the first tear gas canisters flew. The piercing thunder rattled the bones and the earth. I walked slowly and steadily towards the high ground through the chaos of sound bombs and panicked people. I tried to swallow water down my calloused throat. A young white man ran until he collapsed. A few of us revived him and got him to safety. A tear gas canister landed next to me, and I inhaled the smoke before I remembered not to breathe.

That night I tried to sleep in the Bilin ISM apartment, but my forehead and ears pounded due to all the tear gas I had inhaled. Nobody around me had painkillers or decongestants. I read a book in one of the off-white bedrooms as people around me snored softly in sleeping bags.

In the morning, I watched a few white guys dressed in dirty jeans, kuffiyahs, and T-shirts held together with safety pins throw darts at a picture of Condoleezza Rice's face. Why her? Why not Bush's? Why not Cheney's? There were so many white men who had fucked up this world. Why have target practice at the rare Black woman who supported the Israeli Occupation?

Then we all gathered in the unfurnished dining room and listened to Palestinian and white boys make speeches about Bilin, the Israeli Occupation, and ISM strategy for the next weeks.

Later that morning I rode in a minibus with some ISMers to the ISM headquarters in Ramallah. In the living room of the apartment I talked with a curly-haired woman for over an hour. Around us were dozens of dusty backpacks and sleeping bags from ISMers. A couple of small green windows. A hard couch covered in scratchy velveteen.

"How long have you been with ISM?" she asked.

"Oh. I'm not with ISM. I wouldn't join it. I was just visiting to get a sense of what Bilin was all about."

"Why wouldn't you join ISM?"

"I'm just really critical of ISM and this whole model of international solidarity."

"Well, maybe you should join a training and really see what it is that we do . . ."

"Well, I lived in Hebron and at-Tuwani, so I've seen what ISM does and . . ."

"Okay, so, what are your critiques?"

That folks who looked white were more valuable to ISM than those who "looked Palestinian." That Palestinians should be true leaders of the movement rather than foreigners, and not just the way NGOs in Palestine do it, to have Palestinians as consultants. We needed to center those who were most vulnerable to violence in the work. And we needed to trust those who were most oppressed in our work. ISM, in my view, was using the conservative part of Palestinian society as a way to be oppressive inside of ISM and that was immoral and ineffective. People should feel free to join ISM if they were gay or trans. If ISM was to be successful, it needed better trainings. More people who at least knew basic Arabic. A team in which a leader had more than just three months of experience under their belt. That having long-term relationships with Palestinian communities was vital. That the machismo within ISM was distracting.

While we talked, she nursed her baby. ISMers interrupted at times and she responded to them in Arabic, Hebrew, and English.

She asked me my name.

"Mai'a. What's yours?"

"Neta."

"Oh. How long have you been with ISM?"

"Since the beginning. I helped start ISM."

"What? Oh my god. You're Neta? You're that Neta? Holy shit."

She smirked and I laughed.

"Nice to meet you."

Everyone knew who Neta was. She had stayed in the Ramallah compound with Yasser Arafat when it had been besieged by the Israeli army. Had founded ISM. Helped break Palestinians out of Israeli prisons. She was a legend and I had just spent the past hour critiquing her life's work.

"You should come be a trainer for ISM to help us do it better . . ."

"Maybe, I don't know . . . I would probably piss people off."

"I piss people off all the time."

I left the apartment with the two European ISMers. It was midafternoon. The bare sun.

We ate falafel and drank sodas in a restaurant. The boys talked excitedly about getting tear gassed in Hebron and Bilin. "Yeah, this one just popped his tear gas cherry last week." The Swede poked his elbow at the quieter dark-haired German colleague.

I took a sip from my soda. "'Tear gas and a beer' is what we used to call it. Activist Fridays in the West Bank."

"Oh, that sounds cool. I'm going to start saying that."

I sighed and didn't bother to tell them it was an insult.

When folks found out I was pregnant, they asked, "What are you going to do with yourself? A baby changes everything."

"I'll just take my baby with me," I said. "Everywhere. I know women who have done that. Sling their baby on their back and keep on going."

"But you won't be able to . . ."

"I don't plan to take my baby to the front lines of Bilin. But, it is to be said, there are a lot of children in Palestine. Mine will just be one more. I mean, Neta runs ISM while nursing her babes . . ."

Before work, I sipped black tea with mint leaves in Bethlehem cafés, smiling to myself. I was making new life in the midst of war. Someday there would be a Palestinian state, our child would be Palestinian, and Cal and I would make a home and community here. This was the world we believed in. The desert hills. The hot summers and rainy winters. Chopping vegetables on a freshly washed patio under the noonday sun, watching the neighbors pass by.

By August, I had been in the West Bank for nearly three months. The heat settled into a haze. It was time to renew my tourist visa. Hannah, the ginger-haired American who had been with me the night of the pregnancy test, and I decided to cross the Israeli/Jordanian border together. To get a new tourist visa, we had to leave the West Bank, spend a couple of days in Jordan, and then reenter West Bank through the Israeli controlled border.

As Hannah and I rode to Israel, I told them about the last time I had crossed the border with Cal and the wild, sad weeks we'd spent in Jordan in 2004 with a brave mama.

"We were supposed to be on vacation in Jordan, but instead I was looking at the bruises on an Iraqi refugee woman named Umm Rabia, after her brother-in-law, Ahmed, had grabbed and twisted her arm and pushed her up against a wall. She and her daughter had run out of their apartment and downstairs to their landlord's after Ahmed had attacked her."

A week before seeing Umm Rabia's bruises, Cal and I had been lying on our hotel bed in Petra, Jordan, engrossed in a movie, relaxing after having spent the day exploring the ancient ruins in Petra like the hundreds of other tourists there. We were taking a break from having lived and worked in the village of at-Tuwani. We were watching a gangster flick on television when the phone rang. Cal answered.

"Who is it?" I mouthed.

Our boss had a "special project" for us. We needed to be in Amman, the capital city of Jordan, by 5:00 p.m. tomorrow to meet Matt, a member of the Iraq branch of the organization for which we worked, and he would explain everything we needed to know. And no, our boss couldn't say any more over the phone. Cal and I weren't excited about this new project or the heightened secrecy; we were exhausted from working in at-Tuwani and annoyed that our vacation had been cut short.

We met Matt in a busy family restaurant in Amman and sat on plastic chairs eating sandwiches in the middle of the dining room, while he told us about our "special project": an Iraqi family in Amman he had been helping for the past couple of weeks.

After the U.S. invasion of Iraq in 2003, Abu Rabia, an Iraqi journalist living in Baghdad, was arrested by U.S. forces and sent to several prisons in Iraq including Abu Ghraib. When he was released, months later, he became an organizer against the inhumane treatment of detainees in prisons. During the spring of 2004, after the pictures of torture in Abu Ghraib prison became public, he was giving two or three interviews a day to journalists from around the world. Our organization worked closely with him as well. Somehow, he got ahold of documents from Abu Ghraib, hid them, and arranged with the American Civil Liberties Union (ACLU) for him to give them these papers that would be a key piece of evidence in the ACLU's case against the U.S. military.

While he was in Amman, plainclothesmen followed him. He finally approached the men sitting at a table behind him in a restaurant and introduced himself. At the same time, in Baghdad, plainclothes armed men came to his house, while his wife, Umm Rabia, and his eleven-year-old daughter, Rabia, were sleeping. They identified themselves as CIA and asked to speak with Abu Rabia. When they realized that he was not home, they ransacked the house. A couple of weeks after Abu Rabia returned to Baghdad, he was sitting in his car, waiting at an intersection, when, according to witnesses, two men walked up to his car, asked to see his ID, and then shot him in the head before disappearing into the crowded streets.

A couple of months after his murder, two American men visited Rabia's classroom and asked the children if anyone had

had a father killed recently. Rabia raised her hand. They took her out of the classroom and asked, "Who killed your father?" She answered, "You did."

Umm Rabia, her brother-in-law Ahmed (who was arrested and taken to Abu Ghraib after his brother was murdered), and Rabia escaped to Amman, rented an apartment, and waited for their plane tickets to Sweden. Our organization had promised that they were going to be refugees in Sweden in just a few days, just a few weeks; they just needed to wait in Amman, looking over their shoulders for death, pass a couple of perfunctory interviews with the United Nations High Commission of Refugees (UNHCR), and then they would fly away and start their new life.

After Cal and I arrived in Amman and met with Matt and the Iraqi family, Matt left on an airplane to another country, to his home country. Cal and I sat on the bed in our cold hotel room. The heat only worked for a few hours every night. Damp walls and a bathroom that smelled like old men and cheap rosewater room deodorizer.

Early in the afternoon we visited the family's three-bedroom apartment a few miles from our hotel. Umm Rabia served us tea and coffee while Ahmed talked to us in his version of English. "America have no love Iraq."

We gathered in the living room, in front of the gas heater, and watched the television news recounting the latest attacks in Baghdad. But we didn't talk about Baghdad, not really. We talked about Sweden, and UNHCR meetings, and how much longer the family would have to wait in Jordan, a country they detested and a country that detested refugees. Then we would lapse into silence and watch the news, drinking tea and coffee and dreaming about home.

After six or eight hours, Cal and I escaped into the slick, cold night and walked to the nearest internet café. I wrote letters to my friends that I was in Amman, safe but unable to tell them anything about the "special project." I couldn't tell them how Ahmed liked to show off his "name-brand" socks and the picture of his "girlfriend" who had an American green card, or how Rabia liked to belly dance in the living room to my Christina Aguilera CD, or how Umm Rabia was teaching me how to make "wedding tea" and had bought me a pair of jeans, claiming that they were too small for her daughter, because I was always cold.

One evening, while we were visiting the family, Umm Rabia took me into her bedroom, sat next to me on the bed, and told me that sometimes Ahmed hits her and her daughter. I held her hands. "I am sorry. This is not good. We will try to do something."

Cal and I went to the internet café to write to our boss.

The phone rang.

Ahmed was upset and incomprehensible. Cal promised that we would hurry.

When Ahmed opened the door, he announced that Umm Rabia and Rabia were gone.

Ahmed was recounted his version of the past couple of hours.

"Where are Umm Rabia and Rabia now?" I asked.

"Downstairs in the landlord's apartment," he answered.

Cal and I knocked on the landlord's door and asked to speak with Umm Rabia. After listening to her side of the story, we asked the landlord to let Ahmed rent an apartment separate from Umm Rabia and her daughter, but in the same building.

We sat in that little office as the young UNHCR case-worker said to us, "The UN has placed a freeze on all applications for refugee status from Iraqi nationals since the U.S. liberation of Iraq."

"Are you saying," I asked, "that no one can be a refugee from Iraq?"

An Iraqi family in Amman was waiting to go to Sweden, but it turned out that our Christian "peacemaking" organization knew nothing about international refugee law. We had told the family to wait just a little longer and then you will go to Sweden, and we didn't know that an Iraqi national fleeing his home country couldn't be granted refugee status by UNHCR. And if you are not a UN-registered refugee then you cannot be repatriated to another country. Instead you are stuck in limbo in Jordan.

This family was here, too scared to leave, too scared to go home, and with nowhere safe to go and nowhere safe to stay.

"Yes," the caseworker said. "Yes. That is the problem."

A couple of days after the caseworker told us this, Ahmed disappeared. His clothes, his socks, his supposedly important pieces of paper all gone.

One of our last nights in Amman, before Cal and I returned to the West Bank, we took Umm Rabia and Rabia to the fancy restaurant next to our hotel. For dessert Rabia ordered crème brûlée, something she had never eaten before but wanted to try. She started whispering to her mother and gesturing to the restaurant's business card in the center of the table. Her mother translated for us. This restaurant was the same restaurant that her father had eaten in, the same restaurant where he had introduced himself to the plainclothesmen following him in Amman. He had brought back to Iraq a business card like this one; Rabia remembered it. Umm Rabia said "Maybe. Rabia. Maybe this is the same restaurant." Rabia hugged the card.

"Wait," Hannah said. "What happened to them after that?"

"I don't know. I heard rumors a few months later that Umm Rabia and her daughter had disappeared from Amman. Maybe they made it to Baghdad. Maybe not."

After sundown, Hannah and I arrived by taxi to a Christian bed and breakfast to stay for one night. In the morning we visited the Basilica of the Annunciation. We looked like negative images of each other in the desert sun. Their skin so pale and pink. Mine dark and indigo. We walked through the gallery of mosaics depicting Mary devotions from around the world. The Virgin of Guadalupe. The Virgin of the Forsaken. A Black woman holding a child bathed in light.

All the mothers and daughters I had known in the past couple of years in the Middle East flooded my mind. Courage. From the French word *coeur*. Heart. Layla and Yara, Shefa and Kefa, Umm Rabia and Rabia, Daya, Neta, resisting and surviving walls and fences, nation-states and war zones, prison cells and Israeli settlements, violent men and violent armies.

When Cal and I had first met in Chicago he had been reading a thin book on Mary worship. That winter I memorized the rosary and Mary's song in the book of Luke. I could still remember the first verses: "My soul glorifies the Lord and my spirit rejoices in God my Savior, for he has been mindful of the humble state of his servant. From now on all generations will call me blessed, for the Mighty One has done great things for me—holy is his name." And now I was walking through this Nazareth church dedicated to Mary. Pregnant with my own child, who would be born in Bethlehem.

From Nazareth, Hannah and I went to the Israel/Jordan border. After quickly passing through border control, we took a taxi to the dreary city of Amman. Early pregnancy nausea, hunger, vertigo, and hot flashes came in waves. The Jordanian capital was primarily full of Soviet-era buildings, car traffic congestion, and mosques.

Hannah and I stayed in the same dusty hotel Cal and I had stayed in. The hotel workers greeted me enthusiastically, remembering me from a couple of years ago, and asked where Cal was. "In America, but he will be back in the West Bank soon." Nearly everyone who worked in the hotel identified as Palestinian, never raised an eye when Cal and I had gotten a room together, and were excellent at helping foreigners navigate the city.

After a couple of nights Hannah and I returned to the Israeli/Jordanian border. Inside the border security building were concrete and cream-colored metal bars. X-ray machines.

Lines of white and Arab people one by one leaving the building to travel back to Israel or the West Bank.

We waited on hard plastic seats. Border soldiers checked and rechecked our bags and came over to us every half an hour or so to interrogate us again. The dry air was making me feel dizzy and I was pushing a panicky feeling down. It was taking so long for them to return our passports.

"Where are you from?"

"America."

She looked at my passport again and shook her head. "And where are your parents from?"

"Also America."

"Why do you have an Arabic name?"

"It's not Arabic, it's Swahili."

She raised her eyebrow and looked at my passport again.

I tried to explain, "Swahili is the language spoken in Kenya. Sixty percent of Swahili vocabulary is from the Arab traders hundreds of years ago."

"Your parents are from Kenya?"

"No, they are from America. But it was popular in the seventies to name your children African names."

"And your grandparents are from where?"

I sighed. "All four of my grandparents are from the States."

As the day grew late, an Israeli soldier woman walked over to us, handed us our passports, and said, "We are denying your entry to Israel."

"What? Why?"

She shrugged. "You need to leave."

"But . . ."

She walked away.

Hannah and I were stunned and speechless.

We gathered our bags. Another officer walked us outside of the building.

"What do we do now?" The sun had set and the sky was titian orange. Israel was bombing Gaza and Lebanon. This was the first time I'd ever tried to enter Israel when Israeli security was on high alert. We couldn't return to our apartments, our jobs, our lives. The air smelled like petrol and halvah and I just wanted to smoke a cigarette and cry.

Instead we flagged a taxi down and rode the hour-long trip back to our hotel in Amman.

Dar La Luz

Cal clutched a green army bag under the white neon lights at O'Hare Airport in Chicago a week later. A lopsided smile. The last days of a summer.

We moved to Minneapolis when I was five months pregnant. In winter, I spent dark days alone in the house with no one to talk to and no car to drive. Weeks of below-freezing weather.

Cal's parents' friends were renting us their house, and I wanted a home birth. I knew nobody in the Twin Cities, just Cal's parents who lived a mile away. I mourned Palestine: the oven-like heat, the joyful, mournful streets, the life of resistance.

In spring of 2007, I was forty-two weeks pregnant and officially "post-date," according to Aly, my home-birth midwife. We sat in my office talking about next steps. I had spent the past four months planning a home birth. That was why we had moved to Minneapolis, so I could actually have a house big enough in which to birth. For the past week, I had tried everything for a natural induction: herbs, a double breast pump, homeopathy, acupuncture, the full moon passing, castor oil, red wine, spicy food, and sex.

"We should start talking about going to the hospital." She looked at her clipboard and then looked at me, pushing her dark-brown hair out of her face.

I said as I had said for the past couple of weeks, "I don't want to go to the hospital. I don't think it's necessary."

If I was staying home, she said, I needed to sign a waiver saying that I was making an informed choice to stay home past forty-two weeks and that I would not sue her. I happily agreed.

Aly went outside to make a phone call. Ten minutes later, she walked in the house and announced that she had transferred my care to the hospital. I cried and insisted I did not need to go to the hospital. All of my vitals were normal.

My mother, who had flown in for the birth, sat primly on the edge of my mattress, her manicured hands clasped tightly. My friend from Chicago, who was supposed to be assisting the birth, sat next to my mother, her palms outstretched and her lips pressed tightly. They both insisted that I go to the hospital. I was being selfish, they said.

Cal drove me to the hospital, and I waited in a small sterile room with Cal and Aly for twelve hours for the doctor to arrive, while I begged Aly to please just let me go home.

Aly said she was tired and three months pregnant and really just wanted to go home and sleep. She had spent too much time waiting for my birth. She had other clients to attend to.

As we waited for hours, my contractions grew stronger. By the time the doctor arrived after midnight, I was in labor and exhausted. I had already spent the past few days inducing contractions.

The doctor, a small, pale, white-haired man, smiled after checking my cervix and said I was three centimeters. Aly looked shocked; so you are really in labor. She had thought all those hours of me saying I was in labor was a ploy to trick her into letting me go home.

I labored at home through the night, waking up every twenty minutes, every fifteen minutes, every ten minutes, as the contractions rolled across my torso.

The next afternoon, I went to the hospital and labored in a small bathtub. "Look, Aly, I am in labor. Let me go home." I said as she ran the warm water.

"Shh, shh. You are already here. You are doing fine. You can't go home now."

"Just let me go home."

I understood finally that nobody cared what I felt was best. They were going to do what they wanted to my body no matter what. I cried and asked for the epidural. At least I knew they'd say yes to that. At least I'd be able to sleep.

Nurses woke me in the morning. The doctor checked my cervix and told me that I hadn't progressed. Still four centimeters. At this point, the doctor said that I needed a C-section. If I insisted on having a vaginal birth, then there was a chance that they would call Child Protective Services because I had endangered my baby by not following the doctor's recommendation.

I felt like a fatted calf being taken to slaughter.

I was awake during the cesarean. The feeling of my numb body being pulled and twisted outside of myself. And then I saw my daughter. Red skin and closed eyes and oh so very healthy.

On that first day, as I was nursing her, she looked up at me, let go of the nipple, and smiled. She had inherited my dimples. I had never felt so much joy and pain simultaneously.

From the surgery and labor, I learned patience. That all I had ever needed was for someone to be patient enough with me in my home and I would have delivered a healthy baby in our own time. It taught me that sometimes you do everything to your utter best, and you still lose. There is no perfect way to mother, there is just love and survival and pluck and luck.

In late September, five months after Aza Theresa was born, Cal, Aza, and I left Minneapolis on a road trip to the U.S./ Mexico border. From the border we planned to fly to Cancun for my twenty-eighth birthday and then take a bus to the cultural capital of Chiapas, San Cristóbal de las Casas.

I was going there to heal from the birth trauma. To Zapatista territory where the world moved more slowly. Healing doesn't care about clocks, calendars, alarms, zodiac signs, predictions, patterns, convenience, desires, wishes for it all to be over. It moves in its own time. In its own rhythm.

From Aza's birth, I saw that to be born into the world is to be broken from one body into air and land. That the work of being human is to heal over and over again.

One of the first phrases I learned in Mexico was "dar la luz," to give the light. To give birth. That is what Aza was for me from the second she was born, blinding light. During those first nights of being a mother, I decided, fuck the world. We would have faith in ourselves and make our own beautiful world of Indigenous blood and '90s hip hop, of flower dresses and loud protests, of brown eyes and gospel hymns. Of flavorful food and cheap housing. Of fairy wings and pirate flags.

I first dreamed of us driving to the border when Aza was just a few weeks old. We were still in our Minneapolis house. I had put Aza down for a nap that early summer afternoon and was sitting in the living room when I began to hear a high-pitched wail permeate the house. I looked around but couldn't figure out where it was coming from. And then I heard a low rasp, a disembodied but distinct voice, saying the word, "Aztlan." "Aztlan." After the wail faded, I looked up the word online.

Aztlan, the ancient home of the Aztec people. On a map, the nation of Aztlan covered all of the southwest of the United States. Of course, I thought, that is where we will go next. After the last Minnesota winter, I refused to spend another six months piled under gray clouds and feet of snow.

Cal and I packed up our luggage in our compact blue-gray car, and for the next two weeks we drove from Minneapolis to the Arizona/Mexico border.

As we set off for the southwest, Aza, dark-brown curly hair and dreamy, curious almond eyes, had just started teething. She and I had our own love, of biology and blood and birth and milk. I sat in the backseat of the car with her to nurse. Cal bought a small bottle of Baileys Irish Cream and I rubbed

the liquor on her gums when she got cranky. I had looked at
the ingredients for Baby Orajel and figured at least I could
pronounce the ingredients in Baileys.

We arrived in Denver in early October and stayed with
Cal's college friends. We attended a conference of Incite!, the
network of radical feminists of color working to end violence
against women. I loved Incite!'s analysis that emerged out of
their community and solidarity work and was so excited to
meet women I had read about.

The Denver sky was so open and blue.

The conference held its evening and night events in eight-
een-and-over venues. Childcare had been provided during
the day but not at night. When mamas pointed this out, the
conference organizers advised that the mamas organize their
own events. So we mamas spent a fun evening in a bowling
alley. At another restaurant, where folks gathered after hours,
mamas and children could socialize on the patio but not inside
of the restaurant where most of the folks were.

I too wanted to dance to pop music, drink rum and cokes,
and rub shoulders with folks I had driven a thousand miles
to meet.

On the second night, I sat with Aza in a golden lobby of
a restaurant bar while a spoken word and musical event was
happening. I said to one of the Incite! organizers, "You know,
it really does suck to be excluded from events because you're
a mother."

She said, "I think that happens everywhere, not just at
Incite!."

"Yeah, but I don't come to a radical women of color conference to be excluded because I am a mother. I don't think the
other mamas did as well."

On the third morning of the conference, two mama-of-
color organizations held a workshop called Revolutionary
Motherhood. I sat in a small room, on the floor and on chairs,
with a dozen mamas and kids of all ages, talking about the

radical possibilities of mamas in the world. I had fallen in love with these mamas over the past couple of days and it felt amazing to envision with them a mama-centric world where birth justice mattered, where teen moms were beloved, where mothering was acknowledged to be the labor that was remaking the world every day.

After the conference, Cal and I drove overnight from Denver to Arizona and visited with Arizona border activists.

The first night in the border town, we stayed in a cheap roadside motel. Tejano music from pickup trucks trumpeted into our window from the street below. I fell asleep to colorful neon lights flashing.

No More Deaths was a human rights organization in southern Arizona that worked to stop the deaths of migrants by providing water, supplies, and first aid along the border. We visited churches and small homes, Mexican border towns, and hole-in-the-wall sandwich shops. Whitewashed buildings with hand-painted signs. Dirt roads driven by dusty old cars. We slept in friends of friends' guest rooms and took notes on the life-affirming work they did on the edges of the United States.

The dry heat of the Sonoran Desert. The direct sun. The craggy green plants and the thick wild succulents. The sweet chaparral aroma. The way water appeared and disappeared. It reminded me of Palestine. Brown folks living with the desert flora and hills. Vacant and pure and full of possibilities.

We left our car in Tucson and flew from Arizona to Cancún, Mexico, and then arrived in San Cristóbal de las Casas in an early morning mist after a twenty-hour bus ride. We got a room in a small bed and breakfast, walked through the gray and damp streets to a lunch café, and listened to the Spanish Christian music radio, waiting for the rain to end. Indigenous women sat under awnings in the streets selling chiclets and lighters.

In a jazz bar, we met a balding white guy named Duke, who instantly fell in love with Aza. Before we parted, he gave us his address and said he had a room for rent in his house. The next day Duke groggily opened the door and ushered us in. The house was spacious, two stories with walls of brick and wood. Large wooden mobiles hung from the ceiling. In the living room were young Indigenous women chatting in front of a roaring fireplace while they worked backstrap looms. We followed Duke to the back patio and garden. The garden, four times larger than the house, had a turtle pond and ripe purple-and-white flowers. Lush trees and shiny black birds.

"This garden was my wife's joy."

I was ready to say yes before I even saw the room.

"It's small for three people, I know," he said opening the door to a room that was the size of a walk-in closet, "but you can just climb out the window onto the roof. And this is the warmest room in the house." I looked out the window onto the vast garden and the seafoam mountains.

"There is another couple here downstairs. The girl's American. The boy's Mexican. And there is another American girl, or maybe Australian, who is in the room next to this one." He smiled at Aza. We moved in the next day.

Most days the Indigenous girls would take Aza to their rooms and play with her for hours, bringing her back when she started to cry for milk or a changed diaper.

San Cristóbal was sun and rain and light and warmth and chilly mornings and sweaters in the evenings. It was quiet bars and restaurants and tortillas and eggs and cheese and pork; laughter in the streets and brightly painted buildings; the Virgin of Guadalupe and Frida Kahlo and Zapatismo; green parks with benches where I nursed Aza and ate fruit sprinkled with red pepper; covered markets full of spices, plastic toys, fresh juice, and fat bees looking for nectar and rest; golden churches filled with flowers and candles and centuries of prayers and ghosts; dark beers in the evening in a bar called Revolución and live music in the streets where we would dance salsa and make friends. Aza usually falling asleep in my lap around midnight.

In the main bedroom downstairs lived Angelique, a twenty-one-year-old hippie, white California girl and her partner, Mateo, a tawny, curly-haired boy from the Pacific coast of Mexico. They were silversmiths and jewelry makers. She was seven months pregnant and planning a home birth. They flirted with Aza, and Angelique and I spent lazy hours in the afternoon talking about pregnancy and mamahood, stretch marks and exhaustion, circus arts and Lila Downs.

She gave birth in early December in the downstairs bathroom. Her labor moans echoed through the house and the sky was overcast with showers. The baby was born near dusk and we all celebrated. We opened beers and smoked joints and made food for the exhausted mama.

That winter, Angelique and I sat in the garden, in the warm hours of sunset, nursing our babies and drinking tea and chatting.

For the 2008 New Year, Aza and I headed to La Garrucha, a Zapatista community, for the third encuentro of the Zapatistas. La Garrucha was one of six Zapatista communities in southern Mexico. It was the first encuentro to focus on women and was held in memory of the Zapatista woman who had died of cancer, Comandante Ramona.

I left San Cristóbal in a shared van for two hours heading toward the small town of Ocosingo. Aza, nine months old, was tied to my chest with a long black scarf. In Ocosingo, I hopped on the back of a pickup truck with a half dozen Chicanos and Asian-Americans from San Francisco State, and we rode for a couple of hours to La Garrucha. It was a bit chilly, but I wrapped Aza and myself in a borrowed windbreaker. She giggled, ate cookies, nursed, and flirted with our truck mates. We rode deeper into the Lacandon Jungle, the sunset, and I could barely see anyone's face or the landscape. The wind whipped our faces, and I snuggled down into the pickup bed to keep warm, as more and more stars appeared in the black sky until I lost track of constellations like Orion and Cassiopeia in the magnitude and quantity of the stars.

"Wow," one of the college women said to me, "she hasn't even cried once."

"Yeah, I'm bribing her with breast milk and cookies."

I arrived in La Garrucha, feeling disheveled. The college kids helped me put on my backpack, with Aza still wrapped to my chest. I climbed off the truck and walked up to the information desk. A couple of middle-aged Latina women led Aza and me to a little wooden shack near the center of the encuentro. I laid our luggage against a corner and rolled out my sleeping bag.

That night, I walked around the encuentro with Aza. I met a couple of older Zapatista women who barely spoke Spanish but insisted on using the few words they knew to ask me where we were from and if they could hold Aza.

People set up tents around the open plain that was surrounded by deep woods. Bands on stage played polka songs.

Signs hung throughout the campamento said, "Men cannot participate in speaking, translating, directing the encuentro. They can clean and sweep the latrines, take care of the children, and carry firewood."

I sat on a bench with Xmal, a petite stylish Mayan woman I knew from San Cristóbal.

As the Mexican polka music reverberated through the speakers behind us, she asked me, "Do you know why this is dedicated to Comandante Ramona?"

I shook my head.

"She was a woman to be looked up to because she had been in the army and that was the way that she advanced herself in the communities and in the movement even though she was a woman. And so being a comandante, a part of the army, or a part of the good government is now a new pathway for Zapatista women to gain respect in the community. For this reason, she is held in such esteem by the Zapatista women."

I drank water, ate tortillas and cheese, and bounced Aza until she fell asleep. The bass of the polka vibrated against the walls of our room.

The next morning, we woke up, I put Aza in the rebozo, and I walked outside of the shack to nurse her in the cool air. I saw Tara, my ginger-haired Australian housemate, standing next to a mural of amber corn and copper moons. We said hello and watched Zapatista women march onto the central wooden stage underneath a large green canopy. At the front of the stage hung the iconic Zapatista Army of National Liberation (EZLN) black flag with a red star in the center.

On stage a Zapatista woman spoke into a microphone through her black ski mask, giving a brief history of their movement.

On New Year's Day in 1994, NAFTA went into effect, and in response, the EZLN guerrillas staged an armed uprising in the state of Chiapas, taking over several key areas including the state capital, San Cristóbal de las Casas. They declared war against the bad Mexican government and issued the First Declaration from the Lacandon Jungle and their Revolutionary Laws. Major Ana Maria had led the capture of San Cristóbal, where they freed prisoners and set fire to police and military buildings. One-third of the EZLN had been women.

The First Declaration included the Women's Revolutionary Laws, which guaranteed among other principles: women's rights to participate in the struggle, to marry whom they wanted, to decide the number of children they had and cared for, to be free of violence from relatives and strangers, and to be educated. Now, it was thirteen years later and those principles had not been fully realized, but women had more rights and power than they had ever had in the past.

On the dusty center plain in front of the main speaking tent sat the hippies, hipsters, and punks. The Indigenous families from various caracoles and of course the masked women and men from the comunidades. There was a delegation from NYC of women of color healers. Young, international activistas and silver-haired commies. Lots of familiar faces from San Cristóbal. Delegations of radical Chicanos. And of course, Aza and me.

Zapatista woman after woman told their life stories, wearing black ski masks, vermilion scarves, milky lace blouses, and colorful skirts. The signs said that only women were allowed in the covered tent in front of the Zapatista women's stage. And dozens of women (and a few men), Zapatista, mestiza, and international, sat under the muggy tent on rough-hewn wooden benches. I relaxed outside on the sparse grass, laid out a small blanket for Aza to play on, and listened to the stories. The morning grew sultry, and the plain became more and more crowded.

They talked about their lives before the EZLN. "We lived on large plantations and had no rights. We were raped and beaten by the plantation masters and worked like animals. Not just one or two women were raped, but all the women who worked for the patrón. All of them. We could not learn to speak, read, or write in Spanish and had to do whatever our husbands and fathers said. Women could not choose their own husbands. The woman's father chose the husband and forced the girls as young as twelve years old to marry. We could not even leave their house without their husband's permission. We had to have so many children; some mothers had ten or twelve children. Our husbands drank alcohol and beat them, and everyone thought this was the right thing to do. We women lived like slaves. And then the EZLN came and women were told that they could join the Zapatistas and be treated the same as men. They had the same rights as men. They created community councils that told men they could not beat the women; they could not make the women have too many children. The girls had a right to go to school. They could fight against the bad government too. We joined the Zapatistas so that our daughters, our children, could have a better life. And now they do. They have a life that our grandmothers could not have known. Viva la revolución! Viva!"

The flyers announcing this encuentro had said there would be childcare, but everyone I asked said they had not heard of it, not at the information desk I visited the night before or at any of the kitchens.

We hung out with a couple of other mamas and their children, an Italian woman with frizzy dark hair who sold handcrafted jewelry, her two-year-old daughter, and a Latina mama from New York with her three-year-old.

Zapatistas and other Indigenous women smiled and greeted Aza and me wherever we went. They'd grin and ask to play with her. Ask my name and where we were from and if they could hold her. And then they'd bring her back to me when she became a bit fussy. I was one of the very few dark-skinned Black women at the encuentro, and the only one with a light-brown curly-haired baby.

Some men and women, white, mestiza, and Indigenous, gawked at Aza and me and took pictures as I nursed my baby. Tara shooed them away, yelling, "Stop being fucking racist!" I was used to being stared at in San Cristóbal, but gringos and men walking straight up to Aza and me while I was nursing and taking pictures without even speaking was becoming overwhelming.

I took breaks from listening to the Zapatistas to stretch my legs and explore La Garrucha with Aza. On the circumference of the plain were stands where we could purchase everything from T-shirts to patches, jewelry to prepackaged junk food and sodas.

From the center plain, I walked the dirt paths carving through the thicket of interweaving trees. The noon sun had begun to bear down. Makeshift kitchens dotted the paths and provided food, drinks, and shade.

While the Zapatista women marched in celebration and shared their stories with each other and the world, many of the Indigenous men stood in the shade or rambled.

"You know," I said to Tara, "They could get together and provide childcare."

"Listening to the Zapatista women talk, I don't think the men would even know how to take care of children."

"Yeah," I said, "Good point. But why are there so many men here. I think there are more men than women."

"Some of the Indigenous women I know say that a lot of them came looking for a wife."

I laughed. "Like ladies' night at a bar."

Once when I was wandering, a white U.S. American couple stopped to ask me for directions to the main road.

"Oh," I asked, "why are you leaving already?"

"It doesn't really feel like we can really connect with what is happening here," the woman said. Her short auburn hair was held back by a worn pink bandanna.

"What do you mean?"

"It's like the Zapatista women are doing their own thing and they don't really talk to any of us."

"Huh."

A dry breeze rattled the dense branches and leaves above the path.

Cal arrived later that afternoon and found Tara, Aza, and a couple of non-Zapatista Indigenous women sitting on a bench of one of the kitchens under a large turquoise umbrella.

"Hey!" I said, "You found us. How long have you been here?"

"About an hour," he shrugged, "I was just walking around. Figured I'd find you guys."

He had brought his scarlet and black rebozo and slipped Aza into it.

"Do you have a bottle with you?" I asked him.

He patted his back pocket where he usually kept a small baby bottle.

The Indigenous women whispered amongst each other pointing at Cal. One of them said to me in Spanish, "He is wearing a rebozo! Men never wear a rebozo for the baby."

I nodded, "Yes, they tell us this in San Cristóbal as well . . . Cal wears the baby a lot. I need a rest from the baby too."

"It's because he is American?"

"No," I smirked, "most men in America don't wear the baby either."

That night as I was on the open plain, rocking Aza, I met a dirty-blond U.S. American guy in his early twenties, wearing green khakis and a kuffiyah. He talked about the work he did with an international NGO that partnered with Zapatista communities. Human rights documentation and low-intensity zone conflict community accompaniment. After we exchanged field work stories for about an hour—his six months in Chiapas, and my year and a half in Palestine, my three months in Chiapas, and my research delegation in east Congo—I asked him if his organization was looking for more volunteers.

"Well, I don't think it would be responsible to have a baby while you're doing field work."

I raised an eyebrow and then chuckled. "You do realize that there are already children in the communities? Look around, there are children everywhere."

"But we couldn't take responsibility for your child."

"You wouldn't be taking responsibility for my child. I would. And plus, that doesn't even matter. Shouldn't it be up to the Zapatista communities if they want to have my daughter there? Shouldn't they be in charge of who is and is not allowed into their own communities? I mean, my daughter wouldn't be in any more danger than any of their children."

"What if the army attacked the community?"

"We're already here. In La Garrucha. Surrounded by mothers and children. Have you ever even been in a village when the military attacks? The Zapatistas are really a post-revolutionary community. They have even de-armed. It is way safer than the West Bank."

I looked at Aza sleeping in the blue rebozo. Around us were Indigenous couples dancing to ranchero polka music bellowing through the speakers. They held hands and bounced to the music until 3:00 a.m.

La Garrucha those days was full of the direct blaze of the sun and hours of Zapatista women's stories, and the nights were full of music and laughter. It was a celebration and an experiment by the Zapatista women in what their power looked like.

On New Year's Eve, as I was sitting on the ground with Aza in the afternoon, a group of Zapatista teenage girls approached me and asked if they could interview me. They were part of a Zapatista media project.

They stood in front of me, the sun shining in my face. One of them, her black hair tied behind her neck, held the camcorder while another one stood next to the camera person and asked me questions in Spanish. Aza sat next to me. I tried to respond in my newly learned Spanish.

"What did you think of the Zapatista women's encuentro?"

"The encuentro is beautiful. The women worked really hard to create this. Thank you to all the women. I think it would be better if more of the men took care of the children, but I don't see a lot of men working."

"What message do you want to send to Zapatista women?"

"I think that Zapatista women could learn a lot from Black women and Black women could learn a lot from Zapatista women. We are both fighting against a bad government, against colonization, against slavery on plantations."

They thanked me and waved goodbye to Aza.

"I wish my Spanish was better."

Three months after the encuentro, Cal, Aza, and I left San Cristóbal and returned to the States to spend Aza's first birthday with my family. Our tourist visas were about to expire and as much as I loved Chiapas, my heart was still in Palestine. That is where I wanted to raise Aza.

On our last day in San Cristóbal I watched Aza play ball in the garden with the Indigenous children who lived in Duke's house. Aza was half-crawling, half-walking and shrieking while the older children danced around her making animal sounds. A cool breeze shook the amethyst lilies behind the children. A sable kitten napped in the shade.

Zero Stars

I tiptoed through our Chicago basement apartment, two days after Christmas 2008, around cardboard boxes, piles of books, heavy winter clothes, and scattered kitchen appliances. Aza, one and a half years old, babbled to herself. "Shoe. Bird. Water. Baby."

Once again Cal, Aza, and I were leaving the States. This time to return to the West Bank.

Our plan was to travel from the United States to Scotland in early January and spend a week with our good friends in Edinburgh, Theresa and Jim. From there we'd journey to Tel Aviv, Israel.

I sat down at my small desk, turned on the laptop, and gasped. Israel was bombing Gaza. "Operation Cast Lead." Two hundred and fifty Palestinians dead in twenty-four hours. A massacre.

Airstrikes and cluster bombs, white gas, tanks and soldiers, decimated schools and mosques and flour mills, farmers and fighters. It was surreal watching the Israeli air strikes on black-and-white grainy videos.

I emailed our West Bank Palestinian friends, excited to see them soon, as Israel kept bombing Gaza day after day. The death toll rose, and I obsessively followed the news online. CNN, BBC, Al Jazeera, IMEMC.

Militant factions in Gaza had launched lightweight, short-range, homemade Qassam rockets into Israel. While some militant groups, such as Al-Aqsa brigades and Islamic

Jihad, claimed responsibility for the rocket flares, Hamas insisted that it did not fire any rockets, that it had not broken the months-long ceasefire with Israel. But Hamas was the ruling government of Gaza so, in early November, the Israeli military sneaked into Gaza and murdered six Hamas members. In retaliation, Hamas started launching their own homemade rockets.

A few weeks later, in late December, Israel, with a staggering use of missiles, bombs, heavy artillery, tank shells, and small arms, firebombed densely populated Gaza communities. A million and a half people lived on that tiny piece of land.

Israeli white phosphorus gas lit up the night sky above Gaza City. The wide clouds of smoke lifted into the air like a bed sheet hanging on the clothesline.

"It always looks worse on television than it does on the ground," had been my mantra for years. The West Bank and the Gaza Strip were separated by the state of Israel. What happened in one Palestinian territory didn't directly affect what happened in the other. The last time I was in the West Bank, Israel was bombing Gaza. Friends and family from the United States wrote asking if I was safe, because the news video footage was horrifying.

"No worries," I replied, "I've never even been to Gaza. It looks really close to the West Bank on a map, but in reality they are worlds apart."

A couple of weeks later, Cal, Aza, and I were hanging in Theresa and Jim's living room in Edinburgh. Theresa and I had met during the Easter season in 2004 in a quirky hostel in old town Jerusalem. She volunteered with ISM and I was studying Arabic. Long dark-brown hair, a few silver strands, and a sharp Scottish accent. She had also been the maid of honor at my wedding.

Jim, her partner whom I had met at my wedding, was ruddy and convivial. When I was in my last weeks of pregnancy, Theresa sailed on a ship from Europe to Gaza to break the Israeli blockade of the Gaza Strip and deliver vital goods to the people of Gaza. When she arrived, Hamas gave her a Gaza passport.

The week we visited them, the four of us were glued to Al Jazeera live coverage, while Aza toddled on the living room floor. Late into the night, Theresa brewed black tea, and she and I stood outside in the winter mist, smoking long, skinny joints.

As we smoked, she told me about her time in Israeli detention. Before she had sailed to Gaza, she had tried multiple times to reenter the West Bank through Israel. Each time they denied her entry and put her in airport detention when she refused to get on a plane. She saw her refusals as a way to protest and bring attention to Israel's control over Palestine's borders and its refusal to allow activists into Palestine. She went to the border detention facility, called her Scottish embassy, and worked with a lawyer to put a case before Israel about her right to enter Palestine. She stayed in detention for a couple of weeks while her case was being adjudicated. The food was shitty and sometimes the nights were lonely. She lost the case each time but gained media attention to the Palestinian cause.

Our last night in Edinburgh, Aza screamed in her sleep, refusing to wake up. I rocked her against my chest. Then I turned back to the large television screen and watched photographs of brown, curly-haired children, traumatized and bloodied, appear and disappear on the screen.

Still, I was elated to go back to the West Bank. To deep-throated Arabic dialect, amber mountains, haggling for taxi rides and produce, winter rains, donkey-drawn carts, idealistic university students, to the Church of the Nativity and the everlasting fire of the Holy Sepulcher, to city weddings and village resistance.

Theresa didn't ask me, "Why return to Palestine?" But other friends who had never been to Palestine did. How could I explain being in love with Palestine? A place and people that believed in freedom and resistance, in their own life and death, as much as I believed in them. And what you love inspires you. What you love, you fight for.

Cal, Aza, and I arrived at Ben Gurion Airport in Tel Aviv, Israel, in the early morning. After a couple of hours of interrogation, the airport security denied us entry into Israel and insisted on returning us to the United States.

"Oh god. What are we going to do?" My heart felt like lead. I held Aza tighter and looked at Cal. "We should call the embassy."

The airport security said we had to go to detention if we wanted to talk to the embassy. We couldn't call from the airport.

The border security walked us out of the airport to a van. The stifling, sapphire dawn.

On our first stop in the detention center, we met the basement guard. Slick black hair, thick horn-rimmed glasses, hunched over like a gremlin, no older than thirty. He perched on his stool with the prisoners' luggage, watching TV. His head jerked up as we entered the room like we caught him masturbating behind his desk and he wasn't embarrassed.

The guards took us upstairs and said that Aza and I were to share a room with a blond Russian mama, Natasha, and her petite school-aged son, Maxime. Our husbands stayed in a separate room two doors down, with a couple of other Europeans.

On the table next to Natasha and Maxime's bunk beds, there was a gray-blue inhaler and bottles of cough medicine with Hebrew labels.

Throughout that morning, Aza laughed, danced, whined, climbed into my lap, slid off.

Natasha held out her hand and offered Aza a strawberry, a cookie, chocolate, corn chips, and potato chips. Aza took a quick interest in each piece of food and then returned to her games. I gathered the bits of food on our side of the table.

Natasha and her son huddled on their bunk bed. While her son napped, she cried and paced the room.

An eight-months-pregnant Black woman stopped Aza and me in the hallway and introduced herself. "I am Marie. My husband and I are from Austria. Our passports are Austrian. They think that they are fake passports because we are Black. They want to send us back to Austria but keep our passports. I told them fine. Send me to Austria but give us our passports. My husband told them this is the reason that the Arabs are bombing you. This is too much stress." She grabbed my hand and said, "I told them I am eight months pregnant and if I give birth here they will have to pay the medical bills."

She placed her dark-brown hand on her round belly and swayed slightly. "They hate us because we are Black. You have to fight. You can't let the guards push you around."

After hours, the guards finally allowed Cal to call the U.S. embassy. The embassy official on the phone said, "Israel has the right to deny entry to anyone they would like." She faxed the detention center a list of Israeli lawyers who could maybe help us.

Cal asked the prison guards if he could call a lawyer. The guards refused, saying that we were allowed one phone call and we had used it to call the embassy. We couldn't call a lawyer.

As Theresa had described, the guards brought meals on plastic trays to the room three times a day. The best food that the guards brought was the fresh fruit: apples and oranges. There was also a partial loaf of bread, prepackaged hummus, and hot tea. I gave Aza most of the fruit and bread and stripped the cheese and deli meat from the sandwiches for her and threw away the soggy bread. She asked me for chips, french fries, apple juice. The guards didn't have juice, so I gave her some of the tea, watered-down. Locked in a room with windows whose view was cluttered with security vehicles, police cars, and army tanks adorned in Hebrew, she squealed, hopped up on caffeine.

That evening, I turned on the small television in our cell. Israel was still bombing Gaza. The nightly news was in Hebrew or Russian. I didn't see any landscape on the television screen that looked like the charred ruins of a firecracker fight writ on the night sky, like I had seen on CNN and the BBC. The only words I understood were Hamas, Gaza.

Aza started shouting, "Papa! Papa!" while running down the hallway, and cried in front of his door. I asked the guards to let him out because she is crying. They accused me of taking her to his door to make her cry and demanded that I stay within a few feet in front of my door. They turned off the lights but kept the door ajar for us mothers and our two children.

Natasha barely spoke English. I didn't speak any Russian. Through mime and mimicry, in the dark, I learned that she was from St. Petersburg, ran a salon, and had a big house in Russia. Her son had asthma. They had been in detention for seven days. Her husband's mother was an Israeli citizen. They had a lawyer and every day the lawyer had no news for them.

At 5:30 a.m. the guards opened our cell door and announced that my plane was about to leave. Two guards escorted Cal, Aza, and me to the basement.

I looked at the tags on our luggage.

They were sending our luggage to the wrong city, to the wrong continent.

I tried to explain to the guard.

He sneered back, "I don't care where you go."

"But I do. And I care where our luggage goes."

"Are you refusing to leave?!"

"No, I just want our luggage to come with us."

He looked down from the steel stairway and said, "You are refusing to leave. Then you will go back upstairs to your cell."

"What? Why? I just . . ."

He cut me off. "You will be spending your night in prison and I will be at home in my bed."

I returned to my cell and lay down on the thin mattress with Aza. She was restless, so I put her on my chest and rocked her as she wailed. She'd run out of breath and fall asleep for a few minutes. Then she'd erupt into tears again. Every time Aza started to cry, Natasha said from her pillow, "Shhh . . . Aza . . . Maxime is sleeping."

The next morning, Natasha awoke and put on a sharp, red coat and slicked her son's hair with water. She softly called to the guards in Russian, through the small, high window. After a few minutes, she returned to her bed and cried softly, her back turned to Aza and me.

A few minutes later a guard invited her and Maxime to sit with her husband in the hall. The couple smoked cigarettes in between Maxime's coughs for a couple of hours. When I asked if I could leave the cell, the guards refused me. Natasha returned to the cell finally and took a nap.

While she was sleeping, her son started flipping Aza off. Aza squealed and crept towards Maxime like he was prey. He squirmed in the plastic lawn chair and coughed. I swooped down and grabbed her before she hexed him.

After Natasha's nap, the guards offered her another room. Neither she nor Maxime bothered to say goodbye.

The guards finally allowed me out of the room to get supplies for Aza from our luggage. I waved at the Nigerian-Austrian couple sitting in their cell as a guard escorted me to the basement. I grabbed some clothes for Aza, an extra shirt for myself, and a tiny glass bottle of the echinacea tincture. There were only a couple of diapers left.

"Excuse me, I need more diapers." I said to the guard.

"We don't have any diapers."

"Okay, well, can I stop and ask my husband if he has any diapers left?"

"No, you cannot talk to him."

"Okay, but my baby needs diapers. What do you want me to do?"

"I don't care. We don't have any." He folded his arms over his chest.

I pulled out of my bag three of my panties and a few sanitary napkins: Always with wings.

When we were back in the cell room, I tied the panties tight to her pelvic bone and slipped in a pad. She looked down befuddled and asked, "Diaper?"

"Yes. Diaper."

I turned the television to MTV. Aza clapped and danced to the latest Pink music videos as I spread blankets out on the floor and placed her on top of them. Turned out that the menstrual pad only held about a third of her urine. The rest slipped down her leg and puddled on the floor and blankets.

I pressed a dirty, white towel on the puddle of urine and then hung the towel on the bunk bed railing to dry. I changed her pants, panties, and sanitary pad, washed her clothes in the sink, and hung them on the railing as well. At least urine was antibacterial and antiviral, I told myself. Hell, Gandhi drank and bathed in his own urine.

The guards didn't open our door for hours. Didn't allow us to leave the room. Aza screamed for food, for Papa, for outside, trees, juice. Her eyes were wide and angry at the bars on the door.

We stood in front of the locked door and watched the other detainees, Russian, American, Italian, Arab, amble in the hallway, talking and smoking. We never saw the Austrian couple in the hallway.

In the long, lonesome afternoon hours, I ran the warm water and placed Aza in the sink. She played with the bubbles, a cup, and a plastic spoon. I dried her off and placed her on a blanket on the floor. She watched cartoons while I scrubbed the piss-stained towels and then hung them in front of the window.

A couple of times, while Cal was in the hallway smoking, he sneaked to our window door. Always the guards yelled at him to not talk to me.

Natasha, her son, and husband spent most of the day together in the hallway.

Aza fumbled trying to open a plastic bag. "Shit," she said as it slipped from her fingers once again.

After dusk, a blond woman guard knocked on my cell door. "Are you okay?"

"Yes."

She unlocked the door. "You can come out."

Cal, Aza, and I sat together for the first time that day. He had listened to Aza's screaming, above the drone of the Israeli television shows and his cellmates' stilted polyglot conversations.

That night the guards turned off the lights in all the rooms except ours. I hung mattress covers from the bunk bed like thick mosquito netting and turned my face to the white wall. Aza and I cuddled. We both slept soundly through the night.

The next morning, the Nigerian-Austrians' scared voices through the walls awakened me. As I was rocking Aza awake, a short, bullish man marched into the room, and introduced himself as Yacob.

"Hi my name is—"

He cut me off. "You will get on a plane tomorrow no matter what. We will force you if we have to. I don't care about the kid. I will handcuff you. Whatever happens to the kid will be your fault, not my fault. You did this. Not me."

I continued rocking Aza, "I don't want to be here. I am trying to leave. The guards fucked up my ticket and my luggage. And then refused to talk to me and so—"

"I don't care." He walked out of the room, closing the door softly behind him.

An hour later, while Aza ate breakfast on the floor and watched cartoons, I heard screaming through the vents, "Leave my wife!"

"I am pregnant!"

Knocks of limbs against the wall. The guards were attacking the Nigerian-Austrian couple.

"You have no right!" And then wailing.

I turned down the television and peeked out the window. There were five or six guards amassing in front of their door, one carrying a video camera. Then more yelling. Aza started to whimper, so I turned the cartoons' volume back on.

They dragged the husband out of the room. I prayed the Hail Mary for the couple and their unborn baby. They locked Marie in a different cell.

And then silent dead air.

A guard came to escort Aza and me to Yacob's office. From the hallway, I heard Marie yell, "You treat us like animals!"

When we reached Yacob's office, Aza squealed, pointed to the large aquarium on the side of his office wall. "Fish!"

Three large coral fish glided in the water.

Yacob sat behind a polished wooden desk, a computer monitor to his right.

He squinted at me and said, "This is not a hotel." What?

He continued, "Tonight, you will get on a plane. I don't care about the child. This is not a hotel. You cannot stay here." He swiveled the monitor toward me. "I am going to show you a video."

I watched blurry people getting on a plane smiling, shaking hands with prison guards, and then a still photo of a man on his back, his hands and ankles shackled, being pulled out of a van.

"Why are you showing me this?"

"There are two ways to get on the plane. The nice way. And then this way. See. See. You are going on the plane. I don't ever want to see you again."

"Okay, dude, trust me, I don't ever want to see you again either. Good. I don't want to be here."

"Then why didn't you get on the plane before?"

"Because you got the wrong—"

"I don't want to hear it."

"Then why do you ask?"

Aza, grinned at me, "Fish! Fish!"

"I don't care about the child."

"You don't need to threaten her."

"If something happens to her. It is your fault. Not mine. Not mine."

"Fish!" she cheered.

"Yes," he looked wearily at her and his glass aquarium, ". . . fish."

Aza and I walked out of his office. Cal stood in the hallway, blowing cigarette smoke into the window's breeze.

I stopped in front of him, "Honey, they think that we think we are in a hotel."

Cal cocked his head to the side, "What? Why would they?"

Yacob behind me bellowed. "Why else would you be here?"

"No, don't answer the question. It's rhetorical. He doesn't really want to know." Cal handed me the rest of his cigarette. I inhaled the smoke and gestured around me, "I mean really, this isn't a hotel? 'Cause I totally thought this was a hotel. I'll have to do a review for Lonely Planet. This place is getting zero stars from me."

Cal pulled out another cigarette from his pack and lit it. "Me too. This is the worst hotel I've ever been at."

I turned back to Yacob and said, "Zero stars from the both of us."

A few hours later, a brunette guard, her wiry hair in a bun, opened the cell door and announced, "You have to clean room."

I pointed to Aza pushing a plastic cup on the floor, "I normally clean when my daughter goes to sleep. I keep the blankets on the floor for her to piss on."

She took a couple of more steps into the room and watched Aza for a moment, "Why didn't you just ask for diapers?"

"I did, but they said they didn't have any diapers."

"Of course they have diapers, you just have to ask."

"I did ask."

The short guard with the manic eyes who had refused to open my cell door for hours popped his head in the doorway and growled, "Who did you ask? Who did you ask about diapers?"

I smiled and said, "Anyone who would come to the door."

"What are you? Her roommate? I mean her cellmate?" He joked in English with the janitor. She replied caustically in Hebrew. He vanished. She leaned on the bunk bed nodding, "I told him to get diapers for the baby because if they don't then I have to clean up the mess."

While she waited for the manic guard to return, we chatted about her three children.

"I think Aza is close to toilet training, so I figured I'd put towels on the floor and we could start now. I'd rather have diapers, obviously. But . . ."

"Yeah, that is the way our grandmothers used to toilet train. Let the babies be naked and tell them to tell you when they have to go to the toilet. Keep old towels on the floor."

She told me about how her family used to vacation on the Egyptian beaches. We discussed whether we should use bleach on the floor with a crawling baby around.

"Why did you name her Aza?"

"It means 'powerful' in Swahili."

"Did you know it means 'Gaza' in Hebrew?"

The manic guard slipped open the door and apples and diapers and a broom appeared, and a mop and a bucket.

She mopped the floor with soapy water. "Why didn't you get on the plane?"

"Because they had agreed to send us to Scotland. But when we were about to get on the plane, we discovered that they were sending us to Washington, DC. We told the guards they had made a mistake with the ticket. They said that we could get off at Amsterdam and then pay to fly to Scotland. But our luggage was going to Washington, DC. And as we were trying to figure out what to do . . . they got mad and ordered us upstairs."

"Oh."

"I just needed to make sure that we didn't lose our luggage."

She finished mopping the floor for me.

"You are the kindest person I have met here," I said as she handed me the diapers.

She shook her head, "They are nice people here. It is just a tough job. They have a lot of pressure from the higher-ups."

Natasha returned to the room a couple of hours later. Maxime shuffled behind her, his head down. The manic guard announced, "She is moving back in, and you had better get along. You can take one bunk bed and she the other. I don't want to hear about you not getting along."

I cocked an eyebrow at Natasha. Where would he have gotten the impression that we weren't getting along?

Aza was napping; I moved our diapers, clothes, towels off one of the beds to make room for our cellmates. Natasha stood by the sink, breaking into sobs and swallowing them. A half hour later the guard returned and said something in Russian. Natasha snatched their bags and raced out the room, without a goodbye.

I called the guard to the door, "Has she moved out of the room?"

"Yes . . . there is no problem with you. It is just because you both need privacy."

Aza and I watched Disney Channel movies, made up songs to sing, and ate apples.

The room's walls grew navy blue as the sun set. The last moments of sunlight struck the windowsill tracing golden triangles on the ledge like ancient pyramids.

Egypt. Cairo.

My chest filled and I sat up straighter. Of course, we should go to Cairo. And from there, maybe we would find a way from Egypt to Palestine. We had American friends in Cairo, an interracial couple who used to live in Jerusalem and had packed up our Bethlehem apartment and mailed our belongings to us after I had been denied entry to Israel a couple of years ago. They were some of the few people who would understand if we just showed up on their doorstep after three days in Israeli detention.

The little pyramids faded into early night. Okay, Cairo it is.

The blond woman guard returned and allowed Aza and I join the rest of the prisoners in the hallway's stale air.

Cal held Aza in his lap as we talked on a long bench in the hallway, facing the window, observing the mute night. "Egypt," I said to him. "We should go the Egypt next." On an adjoining bench sat Natasha and her husband, exhaling cheap cigarettes silently. She stared at me, trying to catch my eye.

We returned to the room. Aza stretched out on a blanket on the floor. She picked up her rag baby doll, patted the baby on the back, and said, "Shhh, shhh." She placed the doll on the floor, wrapped it in blankets, patted it on the back softly. "Sleep, sleep," she cooed.

That night, the guards turned off the lights in our room at 11:00 p.m. I curled up next to Aza, rubbing her back as she slumbered. Her soft breath against my forearm.

Early in the morning, the guards opened the door. I picked up my sleeping Aza, met Cal in the hallway, and we walked passed the guard station and the vending machines, down the stairs, and gathered our bags from the basement. The luggage tags and tickets matched. We got in the silver-blue van with bulletproof windows. Guards escorted us up the rolling steps of the plane. The stewardesses handed us our passports. On our way to Amsterdam.

On the plane I cried, terror and fear draining out of me.

We arrived in the Amsterdam and booked the cheapest hotel room we could find. A tiny corner room, in the center of the city, with a twin bed and a small TV. Mist and fog hung over the canals and parked bikes.

On our second day in Amsterdam, I stared at the television. Obama's inauguration. I felt unmoved by the festivities. I hadn't voted for him. I had listened closely to his speeches on terrorism and war. He would not send troops into harm's way, instead he'd authorize targeted strikes against individual militants hiding in the hills and towns in the Muslim world. I had spent too much time in the West Bank witnessing Israel's "targeted" killings that resulted in the military bombing apartment buildings and family homes. I had seen this policy destroy children and communities, ravage hope in Palestine. I couldn't vote for someone who advocated bombing my friends, bombing me.

The day we left Israeli detention, Israel had ceased bombing Gaza. As if the bombing was a signal to Obama that they were determined to destroy Gaza, no matter what.

After a couple of days in Amsterdam we bought tickets to fly to Egypt. I visited coffee shops, smoked heavy joints, and watched white boys play pool. For dinner we ate takeout noodles with tofu. For the first three days, I wrote out everything that happened in Israel during the past few days, including in Israeli detention:

> *the tel aviv israeli detention center aka prison is a sadistic and warped place. a netherworld. a place that is considered to be not part of israel per se. the guards are almost all of russian origin kids who see too little light and take too many drugs.*

Aza pointed out every baby and puppy that we passed in Amsterdam. And fish! She loved fish.

I didn't know much about Egypt. I knew that we had a "Do Not Enter" stamp in our passports, which meant that the only two countries in the region that we could enter would be Jordan and Egypt. We didn't have friends in Jordan, plus the city of Amman had always bored me. I knew that there was also an American University of Cairo. That Cairo was a large third-world, international city, with warm deserts and ancient pyramids and the Nile. And that it was Africa.

If we returned to the United States, we didn't have an apartment to return to. Our clothes and books were in storage in my mother's shed. And if I couldn't live in Palestine, then I'd live as close as possible to Palestine in the fabled land of the ancient African empire.

We flew to Egypt. When we approached border control, the Egyptian guard took my passport, glanced at me, and asked, "Is your father Egyptian?"

"No."

He stamped my passport "Welcome to Egypt" and waved us through the gates.

We got in a taxi and rode downtown. I marveled at the bright highway lights, the smell of burning trash, the buildings, falling apart or being patched up, packed closely together. It was January 25, 2009. And we were in Africa, in Egypt, in Cairo, our new, strange home.

Fuck the Police

I swung onto the back of Sam's motorbike, leaned against him, held onto his waist, and we took off through the black downtown Cairo streets. His curly brown hair fluttered in my face. He tangoed between cars and dotted yellow lines. Tall, fat mosques rose over the skyline as we sliced through the last moments of the night. It was late summer 2010, the beginning hours of Eid al-Fitr.

Another bike cut in front of us, with two boys riding. The one in front had a shaved head, and the one on the back had slick black hair. The boy on the back tossed a couple of insults, and they sped ahead. Sam faked a right turn and then sped, pulling up beside them. They exchanged more insults, then greetings, then laughter and phone numbers. A few minutes later they called. Did we want to join them to smoke some hash? Sam looked back at me, "Do you want an adventure?"

"Let's do it," I said.

We looped through the streets. Sam called them back and they figured out where to meet up.

"Okay," Sam yelled back to me as we whipped around a curve, "at first when they called, they said that since I didn't have a place to take you, they were inviting us to their house and we could smoke with them and then . . . you know. I told them, look guys, I am married and my wife is eight months pregnant. And my friend is married and she has a three-year-old daughter. She is friends with my wife. We are just hanging out. So, if we come to smoke with you, you must treat her like a man."

A month before, Cal, Aza, and I had met Sam and his wife, Aisha, in the living room of the apartment we were planning to rent. Sam was from Ain Shams, a Cairo ghetto that I had worked in the year before with Sudanese refugees. Aisha, with pale skin and long, curly dark hair, cradled her pregnant belly. Originally from Gaza, she had studied sculpture in a Tunisian university and then moved to Cairo to work in an art gallery after graduating.

"Really? You're from Gaza? Cal and I used to live in the West Bank."

"Where in the West Bank?"

"Ramallah, Hebron, Bethlehem." Cal said.

"And," I added, "in at-Tuwani, which is a small village in the southern Hebron hills. Actually, Aza was conceived in Bethlehem."

"What does . . ."

"Oh. I mean, I became pregnant with Aza while we were living in Bethlehem."

Aza rolled on the floor in front of us with her stuffed bear.

The house was abuzz with people, including a couple that I knew from downtown. "Is this a party?" I asked.

"No," Aisha adjusted herself in a green plush chair, "we just came to say goodbye to Noemi. This is her last day in this apartment. She returns to America tomorrow."

"Oh." I was still confused at why there were more than a dozen people milling in and out of the rooms. I was yet to learn that in Cairo, when a friend is moving overseas and cannot take all her material possessions with her, all her friends come over on the last day and lay claim on what is left: the blender and filter coffee machine, the nice pair of leather sandals, and acrylic paint supplies.

Sam and Aisha helped translate between Cal and I and the middle-aged Egyptian landlady, who held a blue rental contract in her hands, as we negotiated the terms of the lease. Two weeks later, when Aisha and Sam came by our new-to-us apartment to show us how to use the washing machine, she asked me to be her midwife. Our two little families became fast friends. Aisha's physiological pregnancy was going well, even though she was clearly stressed with worries about money and her family and was constantly arguing with Sam.

When Sam had found out that a mutual friend, Muhammad, was threatening and stalking me, standing under my apartment window for hours revving his motorbike and claiming he would tell the police and café owners that I was a prostitute or a spy if I didn't give him two thousand Egyptian pounds, Sam said he'd keep a watch over me. For the past couple of weeks, he made sure I got home safe and called daily to see if I needed a ride downtown. This was how I ended up riding on the back of his motorbike in the early morning hours.

We parked the bike in front of a late-night, neon-lit kiosk, next to another bike, and disappeared across the street for a few minutes. I waited.

The black-haired boy from earlier yelled to me, "You like drugs?"

I took a couple of steps toward him. "No."

"Drugs" was the same word in Arabic as in English. Like "motorbike." Like "hash."

Sam returned.

"Do they speak English?" he asked.

I shook my head.

"You still want to go?"

"Yalla."

We raced the boys through their neighborhood, cutting across narrow streets and alleyways, until we stopped in a tiny street, lined with brick apartment buildings and closed window shutters. Sitting on the ledge of a building, we were surrounded by half a dozen boys, fascinated by our arrival, telling jokes that I could barely understand, but Sam was laughing, so I knew everything was okay.

"They didn't believe I was Egyptian," he told me. "I showed them my ID and license. They still think I am half-Egyptian and half-something else."

"Why?"

"Because I'm with you."

In the background, I heard the boys saying, "Africano, Africano."

"Minayn?" asks one of the boys again, pointing at me.

"Amrikiya," Sam answered for me. And the boys looked at each other.

"You, American?" the boy asked in the few words of English he knew.

"There is an Egyptian movie called *Africano*," Sam said, "a very good film, and they say you are just like the woman in it."

"Really? How?"

"The way you look, well . . . except for your dreadlocks."

The shaved boy, Ali, took a finger-length of hash, rolled it in cigarette foil paper, and ran the lighter back and forth to soften it. He handed Sam a two-hundred-guinea bill, and Sam tore the tobacco out of a ready-made cigarette. Then he mixed the tobacco and the hash inside the pink bill, poured the mixture into an Othman rolling paper, handed it to Ali, and Ali rolled a spliff and handed it to me to light. Another boy clicked his blue flame lighter and I inhaled.

Ali crouched on the ground. "I feel like I am in an English movie," he said.

He moved next to Sam, pulled out a wad of bills, and flicked through bright pink two-hundred-pound notes. I tried not to watch his business, so I stared at the ground at Ali's tan suede shoes, at the pieces of glass underneath my feet.

He smirked. Damn. He caught me watching him.

"He wants me to tell you that he is the dealer," Sam tells me.

"Yeah," I said, "I got that." Ali, the dealer, gave another order and a couple of pink bills to a boy, who scurried around a corner. "I like him," Sam said. "The other boy on the bike at first asked, did you want sex? But this one never said anything like that."

The slick-haired boy knelt in front of me. "Will you marry me?"

I thought for a moment. "You are too young," I said in English. Sam translated.

"How old is she?" he asked Sam.

"How old do you think?"

"Ashreen."

I couldn't help but smile.

"Kam?" asked Ali.

I looked at him. "Telateen, thirty."

"Hey, boys," Ali said and winked at me, "you better watch what you say, she understands Arabic." He passed the spliff to Sam.

Sam cupped his hands over the spliff and offered me a back-shot. I shook my head. I didn't want to get too high.

So, Sam leaned over me and offered a back-shot to a boy sitting beside me. They exhaled, blowing white clouds over the dusty ground. Then the boy tapped my shoulder. I shook my head. "Yalla," he said, and cupped his hands. I inhaled, feeling his breath push on my lips. I closed my eyes, turned my head, and exhaled. When I opened them, Ali was grinning at me.

"What do you think of our street?" he asked.

I looked at the trash tossed on the dirt path, the discolored brick buildings built on top of each other. Three dogs slowly meandered and hid under an awning. And a couple of cats scurried under the balcony lights. The air was heavy with the sweet rotting smell of life. And you couldn't see a star in the sky.

"The cats are cute," I said.

"You ever seen a street like this?"

"Yeah."

They shook their heads. They didn't believe me. What would I know about streets like these?

Sam did most of the talking. I just smiled and tried to follow the conversation. The first lights of the morning crept down the street. We smoked cigarettes, drank Pepsi, and listened to the city becoming alive.

A couple of more boys showed up. Their eyes hungry. Their teeth wet with spit.

"Let's go," Sam said.

We gave salaams and stood up shaking hands and moved through the crowd to Sam's bike parked on the other side of the road. Ali caught my eye as I walked passed him. I slapped his hand softly and said, "Thank you." His skin shined like gold coins at the bottom of a well.

The sky was growing white. The sun would glide over the buildings soon. We rode out of the neighborhood past the tall piles of trash that were waiting for the end of Eid. We rode fast and hard past the ancient buildings and early morning commuters. We rode through the receding shadows of the night like this moment, like every moment, was our last chance for adventure.

A few months later, on January 25, 2011, Cal and Aza returned from their walk down Tahrir Street to watch the protests on Police Day. Riot cops and black trucks lined the streets leading to Tahrir Square and the demonstrations against the police.

I was editing an article on my laptop in my rose-and-gold bedroom. Birds of paradise dried in a vase on my spray-painted vanity.

"Guess what Aza said," Cal beamed in my doorway.

"What?"

He leaned down to her. "What about the police, Aza?"

She put her hand on her hip, looked up at her papa's face, and said in a low voice, "Fuck the police."

I cheered. "That is great, m'ija. That is excellent."

"We were walking past the police on Qasr al-Aini bridge when she said it, fuck the police!"

We grinned at each other, so proud of her.

Two years after arriving in Cairo, we lived in a three-bedroom apartment in the Doqqi neighborhood, on Tahrir Street across the Nile River from downtown. Cal taught at an English elementary school and was studying at the American University of Cairo. Aza was in preschool. I was a freelance writer. Usually I was home by myself in the mornings, writing and editing, but since it was a Police Day, Cal and Aza, along with the rest of the country, were on holiday.

Cairo. When we first arrived, I marveled at the overflowing third-world city. Like Addis Ababa where Cal and I had visited for three weeks in the fall of 2005 for our honeymoon. Like Mexico City where I had visited for three days in 2007.

Cairo. Full of African people from Sudan and Ethiopia and Nigeria. Full of Arab folks from Palestine and Iraq, Saudi Arabia and Lebanon. And Europeans and North Americans. And Australians.

The streets packed with folks selling everything: sunglasses, flip-flops, brightly colored polyester hijabs, scarves and dresses, cigarettes, and cell phone cases. Pocket flashlights and knockoff pocketbooks. Plastic cups and plastic figurines.

Old cars that spurt clouds onto the sidewalks. Traffic lights that were just a suggestion. Hours-long Thursday night traffic jams on bridges over the Nile River. Motorbikes coasting between planted cars.

And that Egyptian dialect, so unlike Palestinian Arabic. No, this was city talk so quick that the tongue ran over itself trying to tell a story pregnant with off-color jokes, wet wit, malaise, religious devotion, and belle époque songs.

In the Middle East, Beirut was the second Paris, but Cairo was the city of vice. Young men smoking hashish and drinking cheap liquor in darkened city corners and hoping for a better life in this great African city that their Egyptian schools had told them was pharaonic, not African.

But this city was twice as populous as New York City, full of immigrants. Like Arab Egyptians who had escaped their towns and villages to come to the great city and make or risk their fortune. Afro-Egyptians whose families had lived in this land for millennia but were still asked "Where are you from . . . originally?" by Arab Egyptians who didn't want to believe they were African. Full of refugees just trying to survive day by day in a country that treated them like roaches or demons, wondering when they'd finally go home and stop making all this "trouble."

Full of Bedouins from the Sinai, who had been occupied by one nation-state or another—England, France, Israel, Egypt. "We are not Egyptians," they'd say in their deep guttural dialect, waving their hands through the air as if brushing away a persistent mosquito.

Full of university students and beggars, full of prostitutes and gay boys. Full of lovers finding small places, dark corners, to feel love without the pressures of family or mosque edicts.

Cairo: where folks talked politics by way of jokes because it was illegal to speak the truth about political prisoners and police states, about the dystopian present and how insecure a secure state can make you feel. And now, on Police Day, it had all blown up. The kids had gone down to Tahrir and gotten arrested and then had gone back down to Tahrir again and again and again, insisting on bread, freedom, and dignity. Insisting on their own version of paradise.

Meara opened her front door.

"Hey, Mai'a's here! Come in!" her Irish lilt greeted me. She swung her short, bleach-blond hair and led me into the small dining room. It was two days after Police Day, a Thursday night, the weekend.

Meara and her flatmate, Sadhb, were best friends from Ireland who lived together in Cairo. Sadhb, a pixie-cut brunette, smoked cigarettes, loved to dance, and had moved to Cairo a couple of years earlier to teach English. When Meara broke up with her long-term boyfriend (who happened to be Sadhb's brother) in Ireland, she needed a change of pace, so

Sadhb invited her to share an apartment and teach at the same school.

Obada's lean body rested slightly on a Formica dining table. He raised his head, and adjusted his thick, black-framed glasses. He had dark, short hair and a scruffy, thin beard.

I ran over to him, "Oh my god! You are out! Obada, I was so worried." We kissed cheeks. "Are you okay?" Yesterday Meara had messaged me that Obada was arrested in the Police Day protests.

"Mish meshkile."

"Okay good. I was proud to hear you were down on the streets."

"Were you there?"

"For a little bit at the end of the day. Yeah, Cal and Aza were down there too. I heard there were mass arrests. Just hundreds of people being arrested. By the truckload?"

"They ran out of space in the jails. It's a revolution."

"Yes. It is a revolution. I admit I love revolutions."

Meara raised an eyebrow. She had told me she thought it was stupid for him to get arrested.

"I believe in freedom." I pulled a couple of cigarettes out of my bag and handed one to Obada.

He crossed his legs. "I just want to see another president before I die."

"Oh my god. Jesus Christ. I hadn't thought of that. The whole time you have been alive, Mubarak has been president."

"Yes, in other countries, in Ireland, in the United States, you get to change presidents. We always have the same motherfucker."

I had been friends with Obada for a few months. We had met in a downtown café bar, Horreya, when he leaned over to my table, asked for a cigarette, and then invited me to come sit with him and his film school colleagues. I thought he was the coolest person I had seen in Cairo, with his halo of unruly, tangled hair and birdlike eyes. He never talked politics or revolution; he was a filmmaker. If anything, he appeared uncomfortable if the conversation drifted in that direction, scoffing that it was "boring."

Now his hair was buzzed. His dark eyes shimmered as he clenched his arm for a moment. "We deserve good government too."

Meara handed me a glass of wine. "Mai'a, you've already been through this, haven't you? Revolution?"

"Not exactly. I mean, I was in Palestine during the Second Intifada and in southern Mexico with the Zapatistas . . . but I never got to see the revolution from the beginning. So I am really excited for Egyptians to take down Mubarak."

"Yes," Obada said. "Time's up."

Three days later, on a Friday, Cal took Aza to our friend Lou's house. Lou, a longhaired and long-limbed white American single mother, attended the same graduate program as Cal. She and her towheaded five-year-old daughter, Finn, lived in Maadi, an upper-class Cairo neighborhood half an hour from Tahrir. We had hired a babysitter to watch over Finn and Aza while we parents witnessed the protest downtown on "The Day of Rage."

After the noonday prayers rang out over the city, Cal, Lou, Lou's friend Kevin, and I met and ordered drinks in one of my favorite restaurants near Tahrir. The restaurant, decorated with fish tanks, Turkish mosaics, and plastic vine leaves, was usually much busier, but this Friday the lights were sparse and the tables vacant. The waiters meandered through the aisles and caged birds swung from the ceiling. My hands quivered as I poured the beer, bronze bubbles rising in the glass.

Earlier that morning, my laptop couldn't connect online. When I had dialed Cal's or Lou's phone, the call wouldn't go through.

"They've cut the cell phone and internet lines," Lou said.

I sipped from the glass. "That means Mubarak's government did not want there to be international media witnesses to what is going to happen." My throat tightened.

Lou, Cal, and I had worked in Hebron, West Bank, with Palestinian activists. We knew the smell of gunpowder and the thunder of folks running away from advancing troops. "But even in the West Bank," Lou pointed out, "the Israeli government had never shut off our cell phones, our internet."

We had agreed that we weren't arrestable. We would stay in the background, not get too near the police line, not put ourselves in the line of folks who were most likely to be arrested. We had little girls waiting for us in Maadi.

"I just want to observe and document what happens." Lou adjusted the camera strap that hung around her neck.

My daughter was with Lou's daughter, tucked in the tree-lined streets of Maadi, being taken care of by an Eritrean babysitter, far away from whatever Mubarak had planned. Did she think we were thoughtless to be downtown on a day like today, a day when we couldn't even call to check on our kids?

The sky grew mauve in the Cairene neighborhood of Zamalek. Cal and I passed by a television set in the window of a café. They were announcing a curfew. I asked a man who had also stopped to watch the announcement, "What time is it?"

"A quarter till six."

"And there is curfew in all of Cairo?"

He nodded. "At six."

We had to get back to Maadi, to Aza. The streets were emptying quickly and the temperature was growing colder.

Hours ago, Cal and I had lost track of Lou and Kevin in the downtown streets between Talaat Harb Square and Tahrir Square. Usually those streets were choked with street vendors and traffic, but on the Day of Rage, the shops, cafés, and hotels were closed. Windows shuttered.

And those boulevards and avenues transformed into quick-and-dirty battlegrounds. The air, tawny and smoky, as tear gas rolled between the tall, neoclassical French buildings coated in decades of dust and smog. A broad woman in black hijab and shiny robe stood in Talaat Harb Square, waving a large Egyptian flag. One toddler rode on her shoulders. Another child stood in the street, holding her hand, facing down a line of black-clad police officers.

I recognized some of the folks leaping across streets, disappearing and reappearing behind cars and buildings. Some shops' doors were a bit ajar with the owners distributing onions, water, and bandannas to the protesters. Streams of people walked around with their noses buried in scarf-covered sliced onions cradled in their palms. The onions made you cry and offset the stinging sensations caused by inhaling tear gas.

Cal and I had lived out scenes like these so many times in Palestine that we barely had to say a word to each other that winter afternoon; we knew what the other was thinking.

He had a high sensitivity to tear gas; his eyes would sting and water before I registered a whiff. Since we weren't arrestable, his sensitivity was like a canary in a coal mine: where there was tear gas, there were police, and where there were police, there were mass arrests. While I could get lost in a paper bag, Cal had all of downtown mentally mapped out.

As the day continued, we decided to get nearer to the fights happening on the bridges. We flagged a beat-up, white Lada, whose driver was willing to take us to the other side of the bridge in Zamalek. He drove rashly through the streets cackling as he avoided the street fights. At one point he tried to cross the bridge and a stout man with wild black hair started banging on the car's hood with a wooden bat, screaming at the driver. The driver yelled back, threatening to run him over. He cackled again, reversed, and drove us through bonfires, and the crackle of rubber bullets shot in the air, and gangs of boys in tight, shiny T-shirts racing from the police. We made it across another bridge, into the affluent Nile River island of Zamalek. The main street had transformed from posh shops and buildings and rich college kids—to a war zone. Hundreds of Zamalek youth, dressed in skinny jeans and soft, leather shoes, scarves draped around their collars, were pushing the riot police off the bridge and into Tahrir Square. They yelled at the police lines, "Go already, have some pride!" and "Leave! Leave! Leave!" The police answered with tear gas spraying over the crowd.

Tear gas burst open right next to me. I blacked out and fell to the ground. A young man and woman picked me up. One of them put my nose in their palm and yelled, "Breathe!"

"Ahhh!" I screamed as Coca Cola shot into my nostrils. My sight returned. "Shit. Thank you!" They handed me the Coca Cola bottle and led Cal and I to the side of the bridge to catch our breaths and gaze at the smeary Nile waters.

A couple of hours later, we stood under the bridge, which had been our battleground, and tried to hail a taxi. Each car passed quickly, often packed with people and boxes, disappearing into the cobalt-blue dusk.

"Cal!" I shouted, "Stand closer to the road, and I'll stand back here!"

Taxis were most likely to stop for a solitary white man.

A few minutes later one slowed and asked Cal where he was going.

A couple of blocks away, an elderly Egyptian woman, with stuffed black trash bags piled on her head, also signaled for a taxi. Most days, we would have given her our taxi, but the cell phones lines were cut, Aza was in Maadi, and we didn't even know where Lou was.

When we knocked on Lou's apartment door, Lou answered. We hugged. "Oh my god! Thank god you are here!"

"And Aza is fine and playing dolls with Finn in the playroom," Lou said. Finn's blond head peeped out of a tent for a second and then disappeared. "They are pretending to be princesses." The girls squealed and made funny faces and then ran to hide again.

Lou had already sent the babysitter home, pulled out the bottles of red wine, and turned on Al Jazeera English.

She quickly told us how it had taken her nearly four hours to return from downtown, walking and catching rides when possible. Al Jazeera flashed image after image around Cairo and Alexandria, the Sinai and Aswan. Buildings on fire, police trucks overturned, men carrying flags and knives chanting, "Free Egypt!" The country had spun into the unknown. My breaths were shallow and high in my chest.

"Mubarak is done," I declared. "The country is on fire. It is just a matter of time before he leaves."

Cal made sandwiches and the three of us adults watched the television news and the girls playing theater. Taking turns to go outside on the balcony and smoke cigarettes. We put the girls to sleep. And sat on the balcony. The sound of gunpowder and fire rippled through the air.

"Do you think that's fireworks or bullets?" Lou asked.

"I hope it's fireworks, but they kind of sound like bullets." Sharp crashes broke apart our excited conversations.

Those next couple of days, Cal, Aza, and I stayed in Lou and Finn's Maadi apartment. We pooled our cash since the banks were closed and bought groceries, taxi rides, alcohol, and cigarettes. Exchanged childcare and traveled to the demonstrations downtown in shifts.

But for me Maadi was far from our home, neighbors, and Doqqi friends and I didn't want to leave our apartment vacant for opportunistic thieves. So we left the lush, tree-lined streets and overpriced supermarkets of Maadi and returned to our Doqqi apartment. Glimmering, obsidian trash bags and upturned, scorched police trucks heaped on side streets. Our neighbors waved to us when we arrived back. Another U.S. American friend from AUC moved in with Lou and Finn and then they traveled to Dahab, a sleepy Bedouin beach town in the Sinai.

All night, in front of our Doqqi apartment, our male neighbors lit small bonfires and carried metal and wooden sticks to protect their families and the block from looters and from the police turned paid thugs. Cal offered them hot tea and cigarettes and gratitude.

I gripped the metal rail and climbed the five flights of narrow stairs to our apartment. My right knee throbbed in pain.

Aza slowed down for me. "What's wrong, Mama?"

I exhaled and smiled at her. "My knee hurts, that's all. No worries."

"Why does it hurt?"

"Because the police shot tear gas at us and I hurt my knee."

"The police hurt your knee?"

"Well, kind of."

She peered quizzically. "Why did the police shoot you?"

"Because I was on the bridge with a lot of people, and the police wanted us to leave."

"Why did they want you to leave?"

"Because they don't like what people were doing on the bridge."

"The police don't like you?"

I chuckled, "No, not really."

Her small, brown hand patted my arm. "Mama, when the police shoot at you . . . you should run."

"Okay, babe. That's really good advice."

In the midst of all this revolution, joy, and freedom, I wondered if it was a mistake for us to have Aza in Cairo. Our friends, one by one, were evacuating the cities or had decided not to return just yet. As the revolutionary days continued, more of our friends got arrested and beaten. What if the violence came to our door?

But leaving seemed to be an even worse option than staying. The airports overflowed with people waiting for days just to get a flight. Packed in an airport with my three-year-old daughter and sleep-deprived, fearful people seemed an even worse fate than the revolution. One thing was clear, nothing in this world was guaranteed. Living was a risk and we felt safer in our little Doqqi neighborhood.

Freedom isn't easy. Revolution isn't cute. Our neighbors had chosen freedom over security. We weren't Egyptians but, for better or worse, we had made this city, Cairo, our home. Home is what you love, and what you love you are willing to fight for. And I wanted Aza, more than anything, to know freedom is not easy, but it is possible.

After two weeks, everyone around me was getting frustrated. The revolution was arrested. Mubarak was still president. The protests were growing thinner. We watched the TV news, and journalists interviewed Cairenes complaining about the daily inconveniences of the revolution. Traffic was so slow because protesters occupied Tahrir Square, one of the main intersections in Cairo. Curfew was from 10:00 p.m. to 6:00 a.m. At night vigilantes patrolled the streets. Pro-Mubarak protesters were out in full force fighting the anti-Mubarak revolutionaries. Molotov cocktails and slingshot rocks sailed across the edges of Tahrir Square. Businesses were losing money, especially the tourism industry.

In the eyes of my friends, that initial fire was dampening. We were weary, worn out. Tahrir Square was still magical, still a place of freedom and excitement, but the revolutionaries camping on Tahrir Square were feeling isolated. On the local news there was the drumbeat of rumors that foreign agents were deluding the protesters or paying them a hundred pounds a day to stay in Tahrir Square or were handing out KFC to convince the youth not to go home to their parents.

After the first week of rebellions, Mubarak promised to hold democratic elections in the fall. He would not run again for president, and neither would his son, Gamal, who had spent the past few years being groomed to be his father's replacement. "Isn't that enough?" people asked. "What more do they want? Do they want chaos? Why can't life just go back to normal?"

The Tahrir revolutionaries themselves were divided. Some thought it was time to leave Tahrir and organize for the elections. Others advocated for leaving Tahrir and expanding into the smaller neighborhoods in Cairo. Tahrir was a burden, they said. "We need to go out to the people and drum up support for the revolution." I listened to these debates, night after night in downtown living rooms.

Aza's preschool opened back up. The teachers said that they wanted to support parents who were fighting for a new Egypt. One teacher said to Cal, "For the first time in my life I am proud to be Egyptian."

Aza came home from school shouting, "Horreya! Horreya!"—Freedom! Freedom!—and waved around her Egyptian flag as she marched in circles in the living room with a shiny plastic tiara perched on her curls.

I went to Tahrir Square in the afternoons and stayed until sundown. At dusk, the fire and stone clashes began between the pro-Mubarak thugs and the revolutionaries. Activist friends came to our apartment for some wine and hash, Paracetamol and Ibuprofen, for a meal, a place to rest before going back to Tahrir.

I watched Al Jazeera whenever we got a chance. The TV set was in front of the large living room windows. Outside we could hear the roar of the crowds off in the distance. Cal and I explained to Aza that the police were the bad guys. She pointed to pictures of Mubarak on the TV screen, calling him "the boss police."

We protected her, but we also understood that the best thing for her was to know that our world was evolving around us. And we didn't know exactly what was going to happen next.

The organizers called for a million-man march on Tahrir Square. And on a warm, sunny day, a million people actually showed up: the unions, the judges, the lawyers, the teachers, everyone.

That evening, we met up with Obada, the Egyptian film student, Meara and Sadhb, the Irish girls, and Drew and Erin, the Brooklyn kids. The first time I met Drew and Erin had been a few months before in a little downtown corner bar. Abdallah and Obada had just picked up a piece of hash and were delivering it to Drew and Erin. Drew was model-tall and -thin, with curly hair and a dark moustache. Skinny jeans and a torn, white T-shirt. He could weave a single conversation about Deleuze, hip hop, futurism, and Middle East politics, constantly inspired by the everyday life of Cairo. Erin was a pale waif with long brown hair, carrying a cache of strange stories.

We entered the outskirts of Tahrir and passed through multiple checkpoints, ID checks, patdowns, and bag checks. At the final checkpoint, a scrawny guard in a black-and-white football shirt demanded to see our IDs. Obada, the Egyptian filmmaker, stood in front of the guard and said, "No, let me see your ID." Turned out that checkpoint guard didn't have an ID.

"Then how the fuck are you going to ask for my ID, when you don't have one?" They started to argue loudly, but Obada stood his ground.

Inside Tahrir Square, the mood was light and drunk on freedom. Red, black, and white flags waved in the floodlights. Hand-drawn signs and posters fluttered from lampposts. Dozens and dozens of tents of all sizes, shapes, and colors were set up. Parades of folks singing with fists in the air. Street vendors with push carts sold popcorn and pasta dishes, Coca-Cola and Egyptian flag pins.

"Thawra, thawra hatta an-nasr!" Revolution, revolution till victory! "El-shaab yureed isqaat el-nizam!" The people demand the fall of the regime! "Mish hanemshi howa yemshi!" We won't leave; he should leave! "Aeesh, horeya, aadala igt-maaya!" Bread, freedom, social equality!

And then Aza started to dance to the chanting and music. She spun like a late winter firefly, laughing and clapping for herself. Around her, Egyptian boys beat hand drums and sang their determination to create a new future. She called Tahrir the "outdoor party" and in many ways she was accurate.

Obada grabbed my camera and took a picture of Aza and me going round and round, hand in hand, to the Egyptian street music.

Tahrir reminded me of living under military curfew in Palestine when I danced salsa and argued politics until 6:00 a.m., of the Zapatista women dancing polka long into the night ringing in the New Year. In revolutionary moments, life felt precious and abundant and people couldn't help but play music and dance, to throw their bodies into street protests, into the complex rhythms of free voices and open hearts. Their own bodies surprising them by how much they hungered for liberation now that they had a taste of it.

By the second week of the revolution, I was scared of Cal going out by himself after sundown. His skin was translucent pale and the state media had been ratcheting the Egyptian public's fear of foreigners, claiming that the revolution was organized by foreign spies who were paying Egyptian youth to protest.

But I just slipped on a long-sleeved shirt, a long dark skirt, and a scarf over my head, and I felt safer than him walking at night. Because of my dark skin and conservative dress, I appeared to most Egyptians as someone of no importance. When I was questioned by security forces, I smiled demurely and said, "I am so sorry, ya basha. I am so sorry. I was at a friend's house and I have to get home, because my baby is at home and I have to take care of her." And they would usually let me pass. Because clearly I wasn't a journalist, a "revolution-ary," or a spy from a Western government. I was just a Black girl, poor and lost in the midst of all this chaos.

In my backpack, I carried supplies to friends on Tahrir. First aid equipment, Band-Aids and bandages, paracetamol, cash, hash, and extra blankets.

After the first couple of days of protests, the rootless, scraggly grass had been scraped away. Tahrir Square looked like an urban campground. Tents, as far as the eye could see, set up on the dirt and concrete. A hodgepodge of nylon camping tents and makeshift wool and cotton structures, like the blanket forts I made as a child. They sprawled across the traffic circle and onto the wide and skinny streets in the middle of Cairo. In the evenings, I drank sugary, hot tea, the wind whipping and swelling the cloth walls and roofs. People around me talked about how, on Tahrir, the strict hierarchies had been broken. They had a moment of grace to create new rules and new freedoms.

I woke up to the cool, blue light of day. A dozen of us had fallen asleep on beds and rugs and chairs and benches in the ground-floor apartment of the two Irish girls, Meara and Sadhb. I just lay there for minutes, hung over, not wanting to move. A cell phone in the bedroom rang.

I heard Abdallah get up and answer the phone. On the other end was his Sicilian girlfriend, Isabella. She was now in Italy. And he was in Cairo. All I could hear was his slow Gazan accent explaining what had happened in Cairo in the past twenty-four hours. He told her that she didn't need to come back to Cairo. "Yes," he said, "it is exciting, and yes, I think Mubarak is going to step down, and no, it's not a big deal."

The night before we had all gathered in Meara and Sadhb's flat, after walking the streets of Cairo surrounded by the world screaming freedom. In waves, people arrived at their apartment and stayed overnight because curfew was enforced at midnight. For hours we watched Al Jazeera telling us that Mubarak was expected to step down any minute. We drank and smoked and waited for the announcement. But the announcement hadn't come. Instead Mubarak got on the television screen and said he would remain president until September. "Leave! Leave!" we shouted to the television. Al Jazeera flashed to a scene of Tahrir and protesters screaming at government buildings.

In Meara and Sadhb's living room, we talked politics and music, anger and disbelief. Danced to Egyptian shaabi music and laughed. Even if Mubarak refused to step down today, he would. Soon. This was our revolution. We were going to create a new Egypt. With freedom and dignity. And a government that answered to the people.

In 2010, I blogged that I didn't consider myself to be an "activist." I was a poet and a mama. But when the city erupted, I knew what to do. So did Sadhb and Meara. Take a deep breath. Pay attention. Support freedom. Dance like tonight is the last night of your freedom, because tomorrow it could all be taken away.

I had learned in Palestine that revolutionary movements were supported by informal gatherings and official meetings, after-hours drinks, smokers' circles, coffee-shop chess games, artist salons, and house parties.

In Cairo, without police on the streets, with banks closed for days, with mobile and internet service disrupted, we had to leave our homes to find out what was happening. The city relied on rumors, taxicab confessions, town crier–like announcements in the outdoor and indoor markets, and coffee-shop gossip.

No matter where I went in public, I attracted a lot of unwanted, sometimes aggressive, sometimes overtly sexual, attention. Indoor spaces, such as parties, bars, and cafés, were easier for me to navigate, network, and gather the latest news. Like in Palestine, house parties during the Egyptian revolution were spaces of mutual aid and social work structured toward freedom, where communities were strengthened and celebrated. Unlike in most of Cairo, house parties (and to a lesser extent downtown cafés and bars) were often spaces where love and desire in multiple forms were enjoyed and even celebrated. Queer kids dancing and whispering in each other's ears. Egyptian gay boys with tender eyes and bleached hair dancing to Caribbean pop music.

For the past two months, Abdallah had refused to talk to me or even acknowledge my presence in the room, even though we hung out nearly every night. Meara and Sadhb had quickly become some of my favorite people in Cairo, and he had been bunking on Meara and Sadhb's extra mattress for the past couple of days.

Now I was listening to Abdallah on the phone in the morning with Isabella. And I wondered: How could she have been here in the center of a revolution and choose to fly away to Sicily, her home? We were living history. How could she be so scared? And Abdallah, how could he hate the revolution like I had heard him say a couple of nights ago?

Yes, there was uncertainty and chaos and all the dirt that flies up during a revolution. It was as if they thought that revolution should be easy. Should be peaceful. Should just be a photo op of the Berlin Wall falling. As if they hadn't thought about the parts that came before. The deaths. The guns. Most of social transformation looked like the deaths and guns, threats and danger. Sunsets and sunrises pacing out your days. The acrid smell of tear gas. And the tears even when there is no tear gas.

So, she had gotten on a plane and flown to Italy and left her love, Abdallah, behind. Because love is exciting but it's not safe. Abdallah was Palestinian, and he couldn't just fly to Italy. Couldn't just escape. I heard his deep sigh.

"Bahabik, habibti." I love you, my love, he said, and hung up the phone and walked out of the room.

I got out of bed, stepped over the sleeping bodies on the floor in the wake of last night's party, and walked into the kitchen. He stood by the kitchen table and looked up at me. The almond black eyes, framed by the long eyelashes. The pale skin that he inherited from his Syrian grandmother.

Two months earlier, Obada had signaled to me outside of Horreya Café, his face grim. "Abdallah is back." I looked heavenward at the phosphorescent café entrance. "Good. I want to talk to him."

I walked with Obada inside. We joined a crowd of people surrounding a little table filled with the green beer bottles of

Stella. Abdallah, who had lived with Cal, Aza, and I for the past two months, was talking to Asmaa, his older journalist sister from Gaza, Sadhb and Meara, the Irish girls, and a bunch of Asmaa's pretentious journalist friends. After twenty minutes, a chair opened up next to Abdallah. I put my bottle on the table next to his. "So what's up? Why aren't you talking to me?"

Obada's eyebrows puckered, "Maybe we should do this later."

I shook my head, because fuck that. Let's do it now.

Abdallah looked down at the rickety table and said, "I'm cutting you out of my life."

"Why?"

"Because."

And he turned his whole body. Away.

Asmaa, his older pale sister, had already made it clear. She didn't want her family to be associated with Black women. One of the last things Abdallah had said to me was, "We aren't racist, but . . . you know . . ." It was just that it was hard enough being Palestinian, to be so low caste in Cairo, being seen often with a Black woman made him a larger target for ridicule. "Mai'a, you know what it is like when we walk in the streets with you. Everyone talks about it."

"Yes, Abdallah, that does actually make you a racist."

But cutting me out of his life didn't go as he had planned. Because in the two months we were hanging out, before he cut me out of his life, before he got arrested, before he flew off to Dubai and didn't get a prize for his supposedly "brilliant" short film, he had introduced me to his friends, like Meara and Sadhb, like Drew, the tall hipster kid from Miami, and Erin, the lost waif from Connecticut. And in the three weeks he had been away, they had come to like hanging out with me. For my brilliant wit, good humor, and ability to always make sure there was alcohol and hash in my bag whenever I showed up.

And when Abdallah got back to Cairo and thought that cutting me out of his life meant me disappearing from his life, they wouldn't let him kick me out of the motley crew. And so he had maintained the silent treatment. For weeks. This had been us. Pretending that we didn't know each other. Staring at each other but not acknowledging each other. And now it was a February morning and we were hung over and waiting for Mubarak to finally leave Egypt. And he and I were the only two awake. And I was tired of pretending he wasn't there.

"This is childish. It's ridiculous," I said.

He nodded. A slight smile. "It is childish."

"You can't actually cut me out of your life, you know."

His slow smile grows. "Do you want some coffee?"

"Yeah, thanks."

He turned to the kitchen sink and started to make coffee, Arabi-style coffee in a classic silver little pot. The water was boiling. The smell of the coffee and cardamom shook off the last of the vapors from unprocessed dreams. He knew how I took it: strong with a small spoonful of sugar.

As he was serving the coffee in a small glass, I saw the new tattoo on his finger. In Arabic it said, Sicilia. Sicily. I wanted to tell him how stupid that tattoo was. But not that morning. That morning I sipped my coffee. That day we would speak of ordinary things.

After coffee, I took a taxi home and napped on my pink brocade mattress. I woke up and wrote notes about what had happened in the protests the day before.

There was another demonstration planned that afternoon to demand that Mubarak leave the presidency. Cal, Aza, and I caught a taxi downtown. As the driver wound his way through the crooked streets of the Abdeen neighborhood leading to Tahrir, the radio crackled. An officious voice said a couple of sentences. "Wait, what?" And then the same male voice repeated itself. Oh fuck.

I asked the driver, "Did he say . . . ?"

"Yes," he grinned into the rear-view mirror. "Mubarak is finished."

And then the overwhelming roar of car horns screeched down the streets. People started running, shouting, "Horreya, horreya!" Waving flags, pumping their fists in the air. The streets and sidewalks quickly filled with dozens and dozens of people. Crowds of young folks and parents and children and musicians, the pure sound of celebration and alarm. This was it. This was the moment I had been waiting for, not just for the past eighteen days of demonstrations or the two years of living in Cairo, but for the past thirty-one years of my life. The moment when I got to see the people win a fucking revolution. All the sacrifices, the deaths, the imprisonments, the murders, the revolutionaries dying in the streets, all of it. Was for this moment. Was it worth it? I didn't know. But that wasn't the question, really. The question was: Would we take this moment and make the most of it?

We paraded toward Tahrir, Aza riding on Cal's shoulders. All of Cairo running toward the square in triumph. Tahrir was so crowded we could barely breathe or move. All I saw was red, white, and black. All I heard were the chants that sounded like a new call to prayer, or a new call to arms.

We stayed for a couple of hours just reveling in the merriment. Then we headed home, pushing through the throngs of people who were still pouring into the square. I was in love with everything.

At our apartment, I saw online the whole world celebrating with us. Around midnight Meara texted me. The crew was downtown at a café buying beers and then heading to a party on a houseboat. I left Cal and Aza home. Drew and Erin, the hipsters, Abdallah and Obada, the film students, Meara and Sadhb, the Irish girls, and more folks were milling about the expansive outdoor café, stuffing beer bottles in their bags and calling more folks to join us.

Sadhb and Meara loved being Irish. And because of their Irish identity, they had no problem, unlike a lot of white American girls had, with the fact that other people loved their own culture. The Irish had fought against the English for centuries, so they understood that sometimes you had to fight for freedom. Yes, they were white, but they saw themselves in league with nationalist struggles.

We walked toward the Nile, sharing beers and smoking cigarettes in the streets. In the houseboat, the lights were low and umber inside the living room, the speaker system blasting Arab and Western pop music. We talked fast. Obada and Drew wanted to unchain the houseboat from the dock and set sail down the Nile. "Tonight," Drew said, "anything is possible." We were giddy off the power of having pushed history forward. We told old and new stories, of folks getting arrested, getting shot at, making out, dancing, singing, chanting, laughing, fighting, and winning. We won. It only took two and a half weeks, eighteen days, and we had ended a thirty-two-year-old dictatorship in the largest city in the Arab and African worlds.

We returned to Tahrir. At 3:00 a.m. the crowds were still heavy in the streets. I smiled as I looked over our crew, with whom I spent the revolution. Abdallah smiled at me. I nodded back. Yes. This was a whole new world. The night air hung lightly on our shoulders.

He and I climbed into a tuk tuk, a motorcycle that was outfitted with a large back carriage. I handed him the money and he told the driver my address, "Cinema Tahrir," and then his in Doqqi. As the driver raced across the bridge, Abdallah turned to me. "Tell Aza I said—hello."

"I will. She always liked you."

He looked at his phone waiting, I assumed, for Isabella to call.

Yesterday morning seemed so long ago. The sun would rise soon and the hard work would begin of building a new country, a new people. The possibilities were endless. And I was so grateful I was going home to Cal and Aza, who knew how to love revolution as much as I did.

In a blog post I wrote in the days after Mubarak flew out of Cairo:

what i realized during the eighteen days was that there was no one particular role i wanted or needed to play. what i felt compelled to do was understand the revolution. from as many sides as possible. and by understand, i mean experience, get close to, get underneath, witness, live, breathe it. and then be able to respond to what was happening in the moment it was happening. which meant sometimes i was a protester with a scarf soaked in vinegar over my nose. and sometimes i was a mama explaining to aza what was going on outside. and sometimes i was a friend offering a drink and a smoke. and sometimes i was a medic offering medicines and advice. and sometimes i was a writer taking notes and hitting 'publish.' and sometimes i was a photographer with a camera and a smile. and sometimes i was a translator trying to relay impossible questions. and sometimes i was the researcher/analyst reading about the history and the future of the region. and sometimes i was just tired or confused or overwhelmed or scared or cranky or insomniac. but underneath it all, i kept hearing this little voice saying, just understand it. just be in it. so you can understand it. pay attention. pay attention. keep waking up. we have to keep waking up again and again. it's not a one-time thing. to be fully awake is a constant reawakening from that half-sleep state of mind that we lapse into like a habit. that state where we stop paying attention and instead get all lost in our heads in fantasies about the past and the future and the not here and not now. and then we catch ourselves and we wake back up. this is the internal revolution, to wake back up fully. during an external revolution. and both of these revolutions, the personal and the political, are constantly being refreshed. we fall into half-sleep state.

*we fall into social complacency and oppressions. and then
we revolt. to fully awakenedness for a moment. and then
we just do what needs to be done.*

The World Is Yours

Around four in the morning, I shared a taxi with Hauke to downtown. As we neared Tahrir Square, soldiers, in camouflage jumpsuits with black belts and dainty helmets, stopped our taxi and said the driver couldn't go any further. They had blocked off Tahrir Square.

Hauke, a German painter with matted blond hair, and I started on foot toward Tahrir. Every couple of blocks, soldiers stopped us. "Where are you from? Where are you going? . . . It's too dangerous to walk farther. Tahrir Square is closed."

Since January I had gotten used to dealing with Egyptian soldiers, negotiating my way passed their roving checkpoints.

"We're just trying to get home, and the only way to go is through Tahrir," I insisted. Honestly, we were leaving a house party trying to get back to Sadhb and Meara's new downtown apartment, but to the soldiers I left the details vague. Sometimes we ducked out of the soldiers' eyesight and then moved quickly before the soldiers noticed. Other times I played the sweet and innocent African mama. "Look, I'm just a mom trying to get home to my daughter." Even though Aza and Cal were safe at home and had been sleeping for hours. Sometimes we just had to back up and pretend to acquiesce to the soldiers' orders and then sneak around when they weren't looking.

As we arrived at the center of Tahrir, dozens of soldiers sat on benches, their guns swaying between their legs. We took one more side alley when loud gunshots rang out. We crouched behind a parked, dusty navy Lada. Queues of soldiers marched passed us in the streets, then half a dozen trucks packed with soldiers sped by.

I pulled out a last beer can from my bag, said "fuck it," slammed half the beer, and passed the can to Hauke. We scurried into an alleyway. I called Meara to assure our friends were safe. "Yeah. We are okay. Where is everyone?" I don't know any other European girls who supported the revolution more than Sadhb and Meara.

Throughout the revolution, they were welcoming and helpful and opened their house to everyone: sub-Saharan Black students, Egyptian boys from the ghetto pretending they were middle-class, and upper-class Egyptian girls who lied to their parents about what they were doing at night, the kind of girls who wore hijab in the taxi until they got to the house party, Arab boys who barely spoke English, white boys who barely spoke Arabic, doormen and fisherwomen, Saudi-trained doctors, Lebanese grad students, American boys on a gap year. If you were cool and you needed a place to rest and get cigarettes, phone cards, painkillers, a glass of wine, an opiate, then they had it.

When we drank, we ran over our international English. (International English scrubbed out most of the idioms, slang. Instead, we spoke every word, every phrase, more slowly and literally.) And we argued loudly with boys who tried to tell us what was best for us. Five days a week, they were teachers at an English-language private school. I could talk to them about which boys were the cutest and the latest downtown gossip, but also borrow a book, talk politics and revolution, history and music.

We found Drew, Obada, and Obada's brother on Talaat Harb Square. Then the sound of gunshots again. We sprinted to the nearest parking lot. I ducked behind a peach truck, hiding from the line of fire. I looked around. Hauke, Obada, and Drew had disappeared, and I was stuck on a street between Talaat Harb and Tahrir Squares. A queue of soldiers to my right refused to let me pass. Another queue of soldiers to my left were yelling at me, "Go back! Go back!"

"What?"

"Go back!"

"Go back where? I'm blocked on both sides."

A couple of soldiers pushed me and butted my chest with their rifles. Motherfuckers. I sat on the edge of the sidewalk. The night, hazy and orange.

I called Hauke. "Hey! Where are you?"

"I'm in a police truck."

"What? Fuck!"

"Yeah there are a bunch of guys in here with me."

"Shit. Do you know where you're going?"

No answer. His phone dead.

A short, older man, with russet skin and green eyes, approached me, introduced himself. "Why are you here?"

"Because there are soldiers there and more soldiers there and nobody will let me leave this street and go home."

He explained to the soldiers that I needed to pass. Then he escorted me to Meara and Sadhb's apartment a few blocks away. In their living room, about five people lounged on the couch and the floor mattress. I smoked a cigarette on the balcony and watched the day grow light with Sadhb. Morning in downtown Cairo. Deafening car horns and the buzz of generators. The faint acrid smell of tear gas.

Twenty-four hours later, Hauke was released from jail unharmed. This was the new normal Thursday night.

I found an empty loveseat in the low-lit living room. Half a dozen conversations in the humid air drowned out the speakers' music coming from the corner.

Earlier that night we had celebrated the opening of Water Studio, the revolutionary community art space I created in the ground floor Doqqi apartment. Hauke had spent the past few weeks creating a multi-room installation from discarded materials he'd found in Cairo and this was the debut. The studio filled with journalists and artists, musicians and academics, tourists and Tahrir revolutionaries. After the opening, our crew grabbed a couple of taxis to a house party of a friend of a friend, swinging black plastic bags full of green beer bottles and a clear flask of Egyptian vodka.

Asmaa, Abdallah's sister, the award-winning Gaza journalist, sat next to me on the corduroy loveseat. In the smoky, candlelit air, her pale skin yellowed. She placed a mug on the coffee table in front of us.

"So you asked me to be in your book?" When she showed up at the opening, I told her I was working on an anthology about revolutionary motherhood and I'd love to interview her for it. Six months before, she was crying in my living room at 8:00 a.m. offering me drinks from her large crystal-blue bottle of Bombay Sapphire gin. Recounted the story of her marriage and her young son, of her divorce and her return to Gaza City, of her journalism in the besieged land and of being physically attacked and imprisoned repeatedly by Hamas for "violating moral standards" or simply marching in protest. It was this story that had made her a pariah to parts of her family and lauded by international human rights organizations.

A couple of months after that tears-and-laughter drunken morning, she decided I was not the kind of person she wanted her family to be seen with. But she'd become friendlier in the past couple of weeks. And frankly, I respected her story, even if she and her brother were anti-Black, white Arabs, so I asked her if she wanted to be interviewed for the book.

"I'd love to interview you."

She lifted her chin. "I'm not a good mother."

"This book isn't about being 'the good mother.' We are just asking if mothers, especially mothers who live under the threat of violence, want to share their stories."

"Do you know how I felt to walk out of the jail and see my son waiting for me?" She picked up the mug and took a long sip, staring at the edge of the table.

"No," I said, turning to her, "but I do know what it feels like to be in Israeli detention with my daughter."

"And you think you are a good mother?"

"I think I do my best to make sure my daughter is happy and healthy."

"I think you are a bad mother."

I was startled. "Why?"

She continued to stare at the coffee table. "You should be home with your daughter. Not at parties. You should really care for her . . . You are a really bad mother. A really bad one, Mai'a." She grinned at me as she spat out the words, taking another long drink from her mug.

"You think I'm a bad mother because I had an art gallery opening that Aza and Cal attended and now I'm out celebrating while she and her father are home sleeping? Okay." I took a sip from the Stella beer bottle I held in my lap. "But you've met my daughter several times and adored her. So, clearly my way of mothering is working." I inhaled a deep breath from the belly and exhaled, "I'd love to meet your son sometime. Maybe when he comes to Cairo to visit you." My chest and jaw grew hot and tight. That mama-bear anger.

People had been telling me I was doing mothering wrong since I was pregnant. I'd spent years defying conventional ideas of what a mother should and should not do. "I've made mistakes," I continued, "but I love my daughter too much to have you claiming that she has somehow been irrevocably harmed by me. She is immaculate and brilliant and healthy."

She pursed her lips and eyes. "I don't think you're a good mother. But I'll be in your book if you want. You just want to use my story to make your book sound important."

"You know what, Asmaa? You're just another racist and we both know that. But I was trying to be kind to you. And your response is that I want to interview you because you are so superior to me? Fuck you. I am tired of hearing you and Abdallah talk about how the Palestinian resistance is the 'last colonial war.' Or that Palestinians live under conditions that are worse than anywhere in the world. Bullshit. There are African girls at this party who have been through worse war zones than you can imagine. And you think they aren't even worth thinking about." I felt dizzy, the air was heavy, and I was trying to keep my voice low. "I'm tired of you guys using your story as an excuse to be shitty toward other people."

I stood up and looked in her dark eyes surrounded by that pale skin she and her brother were so proud of. "I'm getting a drink, and I'm sure you're worried about what people are saying about you associating with someone . . . who looks like me." I stood up and moved through the small gap between her legs and the coffee table legs. "Thanks for the interview."

The white light of the morning, hours later, illuminated the white walls of Abdallah, Obada, and Drew's apartment. I contemplated the soft focus photos of Gaza on a living room wall. Abdallah had brought Obada, Drew, and Erin with him to Gaza through the underground tunnels last fall during Eid al-Adha to celebrate with his family.

Drew walked up quietly. I had wanted to go on that trip with them, but Abdallah had said his family would hate me.

"Gaza was amazing," Drew said softly, "but I wouldn't want to live there."

I half smiled. "I would."

"You'd live there?"

"I already lived in the West Bank."

"Oh right."

"Lucky for me, Palestine is not Asmaa and Abdallah. I loved Palestine. Mothers who put everything on the line for their freedom. That was the kind of mama I always wanted to be. Hell, Aza was conceived in Palestine." I sighed, "Someday. Maybe I'll get back there someday . . ."

I walked over to Hauke reclining on the couch. "Hey! We did it! Your art show went great."

"It sucked. It all fucking sucked," he growled

"Wait. What? I think it actually went pretty well. I mean, we got to present the art studio and people were engaged by your work and—"

He cut me off. "No, the party was bad. The show was bad." He turned his back to me and breathed into the thick cloth of the couch.

I pulled his shoulder toward me. "Look, I already had to deal with Asmaa's negativity last night, I really don't need this from you right now. I worked really hard to put that together for you. Like . . . you could at least say thank you."

He snarled like a Russian car engine. "You just did this so I'd have to say thank you to you. That's all you care about."

My spine snapped straight. "No. Actually, I let you use my studio to have an art show because you promised to build me a desk in exchange."

He laughed, "Yeah, right."

"Yeah. Right. That was the deal . . . So you'll start on the desk next week?"

He turned his back and fell asleep. Loudly.

I walked into the studio a couple of days later and found Hauke reclining on the couch in my private office, barefoot, in torn jeans, bare-chested. My little office, with the large green windows and afternoon light, was the only room I had asked for him not to enter. The rest of the two-bedroom apartment was his to use as he liked. The floor was covered with piles of papers, the printed-out submissions from writers and artists who wanted to be included in the revolutionary motherhood anthology. I watched as the pale ash from his loose hash joint lazily fell onto my papers next to the couch.

"Hauke, I asked you not to use my office. I need one room that is solely mine to work in."

He turned his head. "What?"

"Yeah, you need to get out of my office . . . Actually, have you started that desk yet?"

He scoffed again and turned away.

I felt that mama-bear heat rising again. I was tired of being nice, tired of white people assuming that their work was more important than mine.

"Okay, yeah, you need to get out of my office. Now. Actually, you have forty-eight hours to pack up your art show and get the fuck out of my studio."

He jumped on his feet, "You aren't serious!"

"Oh," it was my turn to scoff, "I'm dead serious. And since you don't want to build the desk, you can just pay me for your half of the rent. Get it to me before you move out."

He was screaming at me and kicking the walls. I sat down next to his cardboard sculptures and cried. All heat and salt water. Sometimes, I thought, you have to be the mama bear who protects her own damn self.

A couple of weeks later, Abdallah, Obada, and I conversed over lukewarm beers in Café Horreya. They leaned back in the rickety wooden chairs, their hands shoved in their pants pockets.

Abdallah pointed to two white men, glancing around nervously, a couple of tables away. "They want to buy hash."

"What makes you think that?" I asked.

A sly smile. "Don't they look like men who feel powerful when they spend money?"

Step by step, Abdallah and Obada were teaching me how to deal hash. There were the regulars. White boy AUC students, no matter how many fingers of hash I sold them, were back a week later buying more. The expat and Egyptian girls who would rather buy from a woman than from some guy on a shady street corner. The Egyptian boys who wanted to buy from the Black American girl who could get them entrée to expat parties with white girls. As we watched the two men, a gaunt white man with floppy, light-brown hair appeared in front of our table.

"Hi. Ummm . . . Ahmed said that you might have hash for sale?" He swallowed quickly.

"Which Ahmed?"

"Umm . . ."

Obada leans towards him, "Skinny or fat Ahmed?"

"Skinny, I guess?"

Obada glanced at me and nodded. "Okay, cool."

I shook his hand. "Yeah, grab a seat. What's your name?"

"Bryan."

"Where are you from, Bryan?"

"Belgium."

"How is the hash in Belgium? Is it good?" Obada smiled.

"Yeah, it's good."

"Nice."

Bryan looked around. "So, do you guys have hash?"

"It's a hundred pounds a finger." I said.

"Okay, cool," he said. "How do we do this?"

I pointed to his chest pocket. "May I bum a cigarette?" He handed me his white Marlboro gold box, and I pulled out one cigarette and replaced it with a shiny, foil-wrapped finger of hash (about the same size and shape as a cig).

"Can you give me a lighter and the cash in the same hand?" I asked.

I lit my cigarette, took a satisfying drag, and handed him his lighter and the cigarette box.

"Hey, can I have a cigarette too?" Obada asked.

The boy handed him a cigarette. Deal done. Even in a packed bar, no one noticed anything awry.

A year before the Arab Spring, in 2010, Obada and Abdallah were invited to the wedding of their hash dealer, Kareem. Obada shot a short film of the classic all-night Cairo wedding party. Twenty minutes of grainy images of a belly dancer, of blocks of hash on a long table, of a party that goes all night. A hash dealer groom with a broken arm. A film in search of the beautiful image.

After the ouster of Mubarak, as the city celebrated its newfound freedom, Obada and Abdallah started selling hash that they bought from Kareem. As Abdallah and I walked through the quiet streets of Doqqi back to my apartment one night, I asked him, "Why are you selling hash?"

"I have spent five hundred pounds in less than a week. My father would never understand how I spent that much money in less than a month. And I need to rent my own room." He was sleeping on the couch of Erin and Drew, the Brooklyn hipsters, and needed a lot more money to keep hanging out with us, foreigners, with trust funds and college loan money, with lucrative jobs and empty time on our hands.

"You know I can get it cheaper from Ali," I said to Abdallah.

"Mai'a, you know Ali cheats you."

"Yeah," I said as I weighed in my hand the cube of hash he had offered me, "but aren't you kind of cheating me too?"

"Mai'a," he said, his eyes growing wide. "I'm your friend."

"Hmmm . . ."

I was a recreational hash smoker. I rolled tiny joints, just enough to get a buzz, not trying to get really high. On the weekends, we smoked at house parties and in the downtown bars with friends, passing the joint to each other under the rickety tables jammed with green beer bottles, ashtrays stuffed with cigarette butts. Most of Obada and Abdallah's customers were in our social circle, twenty-something, expats, for whom these two filmmakers could jack up the price, without guilt.

A couple of months later, sitting cross-legged on the living room floor of their new apartment with Obada, we listened to jazz music and I studied the pencil, marker, and paint drawings covering their apartment's white walls. Distorted faces, illusive messages in Arabic, geometric designs. In the middle of the living room were a couple of low couches and a long coffee table that was usually stacked with empty cups and scattered rolling papers. When they had found this two-floor, four-bedroom downtown apartment for rent a month ago, Abdallah and Obada had asked me to move in with them, but I declined and suggested they ask Drew and Erin. Drew moved in with

Abdallah and Obada. Erin rented an apartment across the hall. I found a lovely chartreuse ground-floor apartment in Doqqi, a couple of blocks from the apartment that Cal, Aza, and I shared. This is where I started Water Studio and started creating a space that housed salons for the revolutionary artists who were remaking the city.

I made a joke to Obada about becoming the only girl dealer downtown. Obada sat straight up and adjusted his glasses. "Yes, Mai'a! Let's do it! You can buy a 'hand' of hash and we can sell it!"

A "hand" was a thin slab of dark-brown or black hash about the width and length of a hand. We would buy the hand, cut it into thin strips, called "fingers," and sell the fingers.

"You know I'm actually going to sell it at a decent price? I just might steal some of your clients . . ."

His eyes gleamed. "Okay, when do you want to buy it?"

A week later, I gave the money to Obada and Abdallah, and they returned to my studio around midnight with the hand. I gave half of it to Obada, a quarter to Hauke, and the last quarter I took for myself. When they had sold their fingers, they would pay me back the money I had invested. Hauke and Obada smoked up most of their hash, but I sold mine, made a bit of profit, and did the math—hash would pay for Water Studio. I was ready to sell more.

Every three or four weeks, I gave Obada money to take a taxi to and from Kareem's neighborhood to pick up another hand of hash.

I unlocked the door and saw Obada, with his black hair and wild scowl. He lounged on the broken brocade loveseat in our living room and pulled out the hand of hash from his jacket pocket. It looked like a large, thin, smooth dark chocolate bar.

"Thanks, babe." I weighed it in my palm.

"Mish meshkile . . ." He glanced to his right at our small, messy kitchen. "So are you going to cut it?"

"Yeah, later."

"Why not do it now? I cut it all for you."

"No worries. I'll do it later, babe."

"Well . . . can I cut off a piece for myself?"

"Bah. Okay, okay, let's cut it up now."

In the kitchen, I turned on the gas stove. With a pair of metal tongs, I ran the hand of hash over the flames to soften it. I put the hand on a small, wooden cutting board and then warmed the rocking knife over the stove. "Give it to me," Obada said and stepped to the countertop. Methodically, he cut the hand into thin slices, his torso swaying side to side with the knife.

I inspected the fingers of hash on the cutting board. "Good job."

"Can I take this one?" A dark-brown slice of hash in his hand.

"No, I can use that one. Take this one." I picked up a finger that looked like a wedge.

He smiled. "It's bigger."

"Yep."

There were usually a few fingers that were too thin, or too off-shape to sell. I gave those to Obada, other friends, the waiters, or just kept them for my personal stash.

Obada left my apartment and Aza and I stretched out in my bedroom. We watched an episode of *Cosmos: A Spacetime Odyssey* with Carl Sagan and wrapped each finger in a small square of aluminum foil. We talked about the difference between the sun and the stars, between Islam and witchcraft. I put all the shiny fingers in a plastic bag in my spray-painted gold wardrobe. "Okay, all done. Thank you for helping me, Aza."

"You're welcome."

I looked at the time stamp on my phone. "Time for bed."

She brushed her teeth and washed her face. I lay with her in her heliotrope bedroom and told her a new fairy tale.

Her floor littered with cheap, colorful plastic toys and stuffed animals and crayons and half-finished drawings. Sigh. I needed to clean her room again.

After she fell asleep, I texted my regular clients that I had "fresh tea" and I'd be downtown in an hour.

The waiters in the bars and cafés loved me. I overtipped them in either cash or hash, making sure everyone got paid. If the bar was "hot," under pressure from the authorities, the waiters would tell me the moment I walked in.

My favorite waiter was Milad, the drunken portly waiter of Horreya, who rubbed his belly, said lewd things to everyone, and knew everything that happened downtown. Between the dirty yellow walls of the café bar and under the neon lights that cast everyone in a lurid color, Milad saw couples break up and get back together, crews grow up and move away. He knew which boys hustled the foreigners for a drink, which girls always had money on them. Who was walking home, and who was catching a taxi. Who always tipped him, and who was going to try to stiff him on the bill. And Milad knew me. I always made sure that our table's bill was paid and always tipped an extra five pounds. And he knew Obada and Abdallah, the boys who never had money but acted like impoverished aristocracy.

Some nights my friends and I bar hopped from Horreya to Odeon, the twenty-four-hour hotel rooftop bar that looked like an Orientalist wet dream. We smoked joints, lined the tables with empty green bottles, and watched sunrise from behind the high-rise buildings. Other nights, we ended up at Abdallah and Obada's downtown apartment on the twelfth floor, near the dawn call to prayer, where mosquitos filled the apartment. We sipped liquor and sweet black tea, hash, and cigarettes until the night got light. Once in a while, we hung out in the fruit grove of a monastery, getting high and picking ripe bananas from the trees, or at someone's Nile-view apartment, sitting on the balcony talking about love lost until we could hear the roosters crow in the distance.

Most of the hash boys, including Abdallah and Obada, reveled in the images of the underground, the underhanded, dealing as sexy, dark, and rebellious.

But it was the glamour I loved, the luxury: not the deal in a dark alley, but the smoke from a joint blossoming off the balcony and into the night sky as the call to prayer wafted in the wind. The glamour was in the moments of luxurious freedom and beauty. The silver lighter, the metallic purple Blackberry phone, the field journal with an embossed cover, the wallet with one hundred guinea Egyptian notes tucked inside. The colorful dresses, the shiny costume jewelry, the Burt's Bees raisin lip gloss, the Othman rolling papers. The necklace of dried, white jasmine flowers that Egyptian hawkers sold to taxi drivers on Tahrir Square.

"So, Mai'a, what do you do in Cairo?" a sandy-haired boy in cowboy boots from Tennessee loudly asked me at a Thursday night summer party.

"I'm a drug dealer!" I yelled over the music.

He startled and then leaned into me. "What? But isn't it dangerous? Aren't you scared of the police?"

"I don't really think about the police. It's not like I'm standing on street corners hustling." That was what the Egyptian boy drug dealers did, a pack of boys standing in circles in the half-dark evening, high and defiant. Most of my clients didn't know where I lived. Only knew me as Mai'a, which wasn't even my legal first name. Didn't know my legal last name, either. To them I was that Black girl with dreadlocks who was always at the parties or Horreya. I took taxis, not buses, not metros, didn't carry more than five fingers at a time, and kept a scarf in my bag in case I needed to quickly play the respectable Muslim girl to state authorities.

"But Mai'a, why do you sell hash? You don't need the money and you don't even smoke that much."

"Because I like being a businesswoman." I kept my books straight, recorded my clientele's habits and needs, and didn't take dumb risks.

"What about you? What are you doing in Cairo?"

"I'm a journalist," he said. "Trying to do a story on how the revolution affected the legendary Egyptian film world."

"I think I might know someone you could talk to . . . if you are looking for interviews."

"Yeah, definitely."

"I think he's here. Filmmaker who was also arrested on January 25. And if you are looking for more about the revolution or Egypt, call me. I'm a pretty good fixer." Selling hash meant I knew a lot of people in all areas of Cairene life.

I skimmed the crowd until Obada and I made eye contact and he sauntered over. In Palestine, I learned that informal gatherings and official meetings, after-hours drinks, smoker's circles, coffee shop chess games, artist salons, and house parties supported the resistance.

I was that Black American thirty-one-year-old girl, with shoulder-length dreadlocks and floor-length flower dresses. On Cairo streets, I attracted a lot of unwanted, sometimes aggressive, sometimes overtly sexual attention. Indoor spaces, such as apartments, bars, and cafés, were safer spaces for me to navigate without the overt sexual and verbal violence.

Late-night house parties (and to a lesser extent downtown café and bars) became places where queer kids and immigrant kids danced freely, whispering in ears and grinning shyly. Egyptian gay boys in crisp jeans taught me at 2:00 a.m. the finer muscle control in dancing "belly dance" as the bass line of local Cairene music surrounded us like a cant for liberation and self-expression.

These were the intoxicating days of 2011. After we revolutionaries had kicked the police out of Cairo. "We run this city." On the speakers was Nas rapping our Arab Spring theme song "The World Is Yours." We had fought against a police state and won. As long as we were willing to fight for our freedom, I believed, we would win the war.

Muhammad Mahmoud Street connected Tahrir Square to the hated Interior Ministry and was a frequent battleground between the security forces and protesters since late January. But in mid-November the clashes between the protesters and riot police exploded into street fires and gunshots.

One Friday night, Meara, Sadhb, Obada, and I, and more of the crew, were once again walking downtown from a house party in the dark early morning hours when we heard staccato shots ring out. A couple of bowabeen (doormen) told us that the Egyptian riot police were clearing out tents on Tahrir Square.

Those tents had been there since January. They were living symbols of the new Egypt, a sit-in protest by the families and comrades of the martyrs and wounded, calling for justice and the prosecution of their kin's killers.

The next morning, I woke up at Meara and Sadhb's apartment and found out from Twitter that the police had beaten the protesters, destroyed the tents, and piled bodies of the dead to the side like the corpses were just another pile of trash on the Cairo streets.

Parliamentary elections had been called. Half of Tahrir was celebrating and cheering the upcoming elections, while the other half was half a block away fighting against the police and patching up wounded bodies. Some activists, especially those who supported the Muslim Brotherhood, were excited to vote in the elections. Others said that voting in the elections was a farce, that there could be no free elections while the police were killing and abusing protesters.

That Saturday afternoon, thousands of people were fighting near Tahrir. I was working in my studio when Cal called me to ask if I would hang out with Aza while he went down to Tahrir.

"Yeah, sure, no problem."

He arrived at the studio with Aza, wearing a long-sleeved black shirt and cargo pants, an old bandanna, and a small water bottle crammed into his pockets.

"Do you have onions?" I asked.

"No, I was going to pick up one on the way."

"I think we have one in the kitchen. Do you want it?"

"Yeah." I went to the kitchen, washed a knife, and cut a large yellow onion into quarters.

He took the onion pieces and wrapped them in his bandanna. "I'll be gone for like one or two hours."

"No problem, have fun."

Aza and I drew fairies on the back of used printer paper and bobbed our heads along to Rihanna and Beyoncé YouTube videos. Her bouncing curls glowed in the golden-hour light.

Around sunset, I called Mo, a friend who lived near Muhammad Mahmoud Street.

"Hey, Mai'a, how are you? Where are you?"

"I'm good. I'm in Doqqi. Were you on Tahrir last night?"

"Yeah, we were there. The police were brutal. Worse than you've ever seen. I finally managed to get a few hours of sleep this afternoon. Just woke up. Going to get something to eat and then go back out to protests."

"Maybe I'll come over in a couple of hours."

"Cool. Be careful. It's Revolution 2.0 out there."

I first met Mo, broad-jawed and wistful, in Horreya, in late spring, because he was looking for hash. He had just returned from Benghazi, Libya, translating for news agencies. His mother was Egyptian, but he'd grown up in New Zealand and now was an undergrad at AUC. But unlike most AUC students, when the revolution started, he threw himself into Tahrir, rather than fleeing the country.

Autumn nights I ended up at Mo's new apartment because it was only a block from Horreya. The walls were stained white and decorated with random pieces of furniture. He shared it with Kelly, his northern California girlfriend, and Omar, his Egyptian-American best friend.

Cal returned, flushed and beatific. "Hey."

"Hey, Papa! How was it?" I asked.

He blinked, widened his eyes, and exhaled softly. "It's intense . . . There are so many people out . . . Lots of tear gas, but I didn't see a lot of police."

"Wow, was the tear gas from the protesters, then?"

"No . . . You want to go out?"

"Yeah, I'll go out in like thirty minutes. Was it hard getting a taxi?"

"Not really. I'll take Aza back home . . . Come on, Aza, let's make dinner."

After they left, I grabbed my mini-backpack and threw hash, rolling papers, cigarettes, a black bandanna, a sliced onion, Echinacea tablets and pseudoephedrine, a water bottle, a Pepsi bottle, my phone, a small notepad, and my wallet inside.

Inside Mo's flat, the lights were dim. He greeted me with a smile as he picked up a large spray bottle and shook it vigorously. I placed a finger of hash on the table, and the boys and Omar held the lighter flame under the hash, crumpled the heated hash beneath their fingers, and spread it out on the long rolling papers. "Thanks, Mai'a."

Kelly balanced on the edge of the bed. "The boys are going out to support the resistance. Mo says it's too dangerous for me to go out." She giggled. "He's so protective."

"What are the spray bottles for?"

"It's a mixture of antacid and water for the tear gas."

"Oh. I usually use Pepsi and onions," I said.

"Really?"

"Yeah, you snort the Pepsi and then breathe into the onion."

"I have never heard of that."

"I'm part of the look-out," Kelly said. "We go to the roof of the building and text what the conditions look like from the bird's eye."

Mo handed me a white dust mask, "That's right, you worked in Palestine, right? You want to come out with us tonight?"

"Sure. Let me just take my pseudoephedrine."

"Your what?"

"It's like cold medicine. I take it before I have to be tear gassed. Keeps my sinuses from getting clogged . . . You want a couple? The package says to take one or two, but I normally take three."

He stretched his palm out. I opened my backpack and punched a couple of pills from the foil wrapper.

"Anyone else?"

Isslam reached out his hand.

"Mai'a, you don't want to go with me to the roof?" Kelly asked.

"No, I'd rather be on the streets."

A few minutes later, six of us (five Egyptian boys and me) hit the streets. We split into three groups to cover different parts of the battleground around Muhammad Mahmoud Street. Mo partnered up with me and we advanced toward the bright fires a couple of blocks away. Molotov cocktails sailed across the flames, then smashed open on impact and a blaze of flames leapt into the air. Smoke wafted up to the street balconies, with hung clothes blowing like flags in the breeze.

The smell of human sweat surged passed us. We sprayed the peach-colored antacid mix into boys and grown men's inflamed eye sockets. Cooled their faces with wet paper towels. Their expression distorted by the pain and the darkness. They took long sips from the water bottle, splashing the water over their lips. And then they marched back to trench warfare, slowly pushing back police lines.

Mo and I, in front of the tire fires, surrounded by the yelps of Ultras, the football hooligans turned street fighters, sporting dark hoodies and dark jeans, waving sticks, rocks, bottles in their hands. We watched the boys set up new barricades against the police. Breathed in rhythm with the Ultras' chants, rhythms, the crackle of the fire, the occasional cool breeze, and the cloying, caustic smell of burning trash and rubber. He held my hand for a moment and we stared into the flames. Silhouettes of lean boys in front of us.

The last time I'd seen my father, he stood in the foyer of my mother's house. The front door was open and his body was in midnight silhouette against the midday autumn light. The day before had been my twenty-fourth birthday, and instead of wishing me happy birthday I heard him on the phone with my mother encouraging her not to take me out to dinner to celebrate. He had spent the past couple of weeks giving me the silent treatment because he claimed I had stolen his video camera, taken it to Palestine on my first delegation, and lost it there. I had never done that. After months of sleeping on my mother's couch, she had finally asked him to leave and I was relieved to see him go, with his heavy energy and chain smoking. I stood on the bottom of the stairs and we looked at each other for a moment before he walked out the door.

He had died seven years later in the hot, dry summer of 2010. His body was found in his southern California apartment three days after he passed. I hadn't spoken to him since 2003.

After he died, sometimes, I'd hear his voice whispering in my ear like fire, raspy and soft with sharp edges. "Take your freedom and joy wherever you can, girl. Enjoy your paradise as long as it lasts. Don't play anyone's game but your own."

I wondered what he'd think of the tire fires and tear gas, the Molotov cocktails and police riot gear. Would he understand how important this struggle was for African liberation? This desire to create a new paradise. Or would he be angry that I was taking risks once again for people who didn't really care about me?

The Brotherhood decided, after a couple of days of protesting the police, to withdraw their protests and support the parliamentary elections. They were the largest and oldest political party in Egypt and were pretty much guaranteed to gain a plurality, if not a majority, of the parliamentary seats. And with their win would come a deepening of the conservative and the counterrevolutionary forces in Egyptian society. The same Brotherhood had refused to join the uprising in late January and only supported the revolution when it became clear that Western governments were willing to see Mubarak be ousted and the uprising succeed.

For many activists, the Brotherhood had betrayed them by participating in the elections, rather than joining the street fights against the police, and the military, in defense of the martyrs and wounded of Tahrir.

The battles on Muhammad Mahmoud raged on. Over those days and nights, I visited all the apartments of street activists and artists I knew and dropped off free fingers of hash and first-aid supplies and gathered information about the resistance. We talked about tactics that were working and the ones that the security forces were anticipating. The number of dead and injured. Many said that the police were being so violent because the revolutionaries had humiliated them earlier this year when we kicked them out of Cairo.

Some nights, I went out to Muhammad Mahmoud by myself, dressed in a white hijab, a red-striped hoodie, and dark-gray cargo pants, with a dark-blue small backpack. Medics, shop owners, activists who were also on the streets with gauzes and gloves, face masks, and water were ready to assist when the next wave of tear gas poured over us like lightning and fog. The gas-lit street nights as smoked rolled down the labyrinthine streets of downtown Cairo. We collected basic medical supplies for the doctors and nurses working long into the night. The wail of motorbike ambulances driving from Muhammad Mahmoud to the makeshift tent clinics set up in Tahrir Square became the constant background.

The street vendors that had been selling the "revolutionary swag" of red, black, and white scarves, key chains, hats, and ribbons now also sold gas masks, Ace bandages, and eye patches. Dozens of young men strode down the street with white eye patches, in solidarity with the victims of police snipers.

These battles were proof that history had not ended in February with the ouster of Mubarak. That revolution was not a onetime event. Every day we were going to bend the world a bit more toward justice.

I'd do a couple of hours of duty as a street medic and journalist, then I'd go to Stella bar a couple of streets from Tahrir. Sometimes I'd see a couple of white boys I knew. They posted blogs and Facebook posts about "the action" downtown, but their photos were usually of the daytime, not of night. Sometimes I'd text one of them after sundown to see if they wanted to go out with me near the front lines to do street medic work, but they never did. It was Mo and the Egyptian boys that thought the fight was worth fighting. It was the Ultras, the football fans that had spent the past two years fighting off the police and knew tactics and strategies for pushing the police away, who howled protest slogans for freedom and justice. I watched them and learned which streets were the safest to go down, when to stand and when to run, how to out-maneuver the police

In the mornings, when I awoke, the skin on my arms and chest stung from the poison gas from the night before. Rumors said that Egypt was using a new type of tear gas that was illegal under international law.

Security forces killed at least fifty protesters. Police snipers hidden on roofs blinded dozens more. Over three hundred people were wounded in the street battles.

We lost Revolution 2.0. The parliamentary elections went forward. The police returned en masse to the Cairo streets. Larger political forces, smoky backroom deals, and optimistic betrayals ruled the day.

But, the street artists recreated the "security walls" on Muhammad Mahmoud and around the Interior Ministry, in the voices and images of the martyrs and the survivors. Every day more and more murals appeared, recording the revolution on the concrete slabs around the Interior Ministry. A mix of Egyptian revolution slogans and primary-colored Arabic graffiti, images of ancient pharaohs with names of the murdered painted across the dead kings' faces. Insults against Field Marshal Tantawi. Riffs on the Egyptian folk hajj drawings, depicting pilgrims' return from Mecca. Jokes and puns about Mubarak and other public figures. Portraits of the wounded, scenes of police beating protesters, and a spray-painted stencil Queen Nefertiti wearing a gas mask.

On these walls, we signed our names and mourned and celebrated and cleaved to the bright dreams of the Arab Spring.

Ultraviolet Spring

I heard banging at the front door. A neighbor from downstairs was yelling, gesturing violently. Some of the Arab Egyptian boys went to reason with him.

"He says we can't have a party. The music's too loud."

"That's weird. I can barely hear the music on the patio when I'm in the kitchen," I sighed. "Okay, turn down the music for a bit."

"It's okay, everyone!" I announced. "We'll just chill for a few minutes."

For the past couple of hours, I was gliding through the hallways and kitchen, getting cups and ice and extra chairs, greeting guests, distributing hash and tobacco, directing folks to the bathroom and the large, peacock-green patio that was roofed over with dried palm fronds, like a Red Sea bungalow. In the living room, black and gilded couches and a long wooden table.

When the clashes on Muhammad Mahmoud died down, a couple of American friends, Ani, a Black AUC student from Compton, and Michael, a tall and shy English teacher from Massachusetts, and I threw a party in Ani's large fourth-floor apartment in Doqqi. "It's been so tense out in the streets. Let's do something to relieve some stress." Now it was midnight, the apartment filled with people.

Twenty minutes after the downstairs neighbor's ultimatum, Ani screamed, "Turn down the music! Turn down the fucking music!"

I ran into the living room. A throng of boys gathered in front of the door.

Someone turned off the music.

Michael's face flushed. "He says we have to get all these people out of here."

"That's ridiculous. We can invite friends to our apartment."

Another loud knock on the door. "Everyone get out! Get out now! He has a knife! Get out now!"

Everything was chaos. People streaming through the living room and out of the front door. Ani still screaming. The pungent smell of fear and perspiration.

I sat down on a dining room chair and watched the rush and noise like it was a dream.

First rule of working in crisis zones, when people around you are panicking, you must slow down. Step out of the panic. Assess the situation. Work out what to do next.

Ani's thin, black hair disarrayed. "Mai'a! Mai'a! Oh my god! I can't believe this is happening? Did you see he had a knife?"

I looked her in the eye. "It's okay. Calm down."

Her face relaxed finally.

I called Drew. "Where are you guys?"

"We're outside. We're going to go home."

"Oh please, come back upstairs."

"Yeah, Mai'a, I think we're going to go now. I'll talk to you tomorrow."

"But . . ."

He hung up.

Three stocky thugs in the living room, brandishing large knives. Grunting in Arabic.

Then in a flash they were gone.

And so was my Mac laptop and my Blackberry phone.

A few people remained after the party, Ani and Michael, a few Egyptian boys I knew from downtown, and Ayomide, a Black American guy.

Ayomide, a Black American friend, was bleeding badly in his hand. Michael wrapped his hand in toilet paper. The thugs had cut his palm three times when he struggled to stop them.

An hour later, I knocked on the filmmakers Obada and Abdallah's twelfth floor apartment door.

"Who is it?" said Abdallah's low voice.

"It's me. Mai'a."

I took a deep breath and smiled as he opened the door. Never let them see you shaking, I reminded myself.

"Marhaba, darling." We kissed cheeks. Meara and Obada on one couch. Sadhb perched on a high table with her new Egyptian boy lover. Isabella, Abdallah's Italian girlfriend, in the kitchen boiling water for tea.

"How are you?"

"I'm good, Abdallah. I'm good."

Obada and I exchanged salaams. "You okay?"

"Yeah. I'm okay."

"Good, I'm glad you didn't get hurt."

"Thanks."

"What happened?"

"I'm still not sure exactly, but . . ." I told them what had occurred after they left.

Two days later, Abdallah and I were drinking whiskey on his couch. "When I opened the door, you looked so calm and beautiful. Not upset or angry. Beautiful."

"There was no need to panic," I said. "If people stayed calm and sat down and stopped fucking yelling, then we could stick together and stay safe. But instead, our friends just left me there even when I asked them to stay."

"Because they were scared," Abdallah said.

"So they left me to deal with armed men on my own? Leaving me to do what? Fight off men with machetes?"

Tears started to fall out of my eyes. "Sorry," I said and tried to laugh. He handed me some napkins. "Of course. You swallow your pain."

A few days later, Drew, my tall Brooklyn hipster friend, leaned his elbow on the small table. It wobbled slightly. He pulled a cigarette out and offered it to me.

I watched the regulars playing chess and drinking coffee in tiny cloudy glasses. "I like it when it's empty like this."

For the past couple of weeks, a series of white people at parties and cafés insisted on approaching me to tell me that there was no racism in Egypt. I should just admit that Black people were treated like everyone else. Really, it was white people who were the real victims of racism. All of this in response to a three-hundred-word blog post riffing on a blog post by Josh, a white American English teacher in Cairo.

I had met Josh that summer. Abdallah and I were sitting in Horreya at the table nearest to the door, fingers of hash in our pockets. "Our office," Abdallah dubbed it.

Josh came up and wanted some hash, "I don't have money on me now. Can I get it to you later?"

I sized up the floppy, light-brown hair and baby cheeks and asked Abdallah. "He's good?"

"Yeah."

A week later, Josh came to my table and handed me the money.

We hung out a few times after that. Once Abdallah, Josh, and I hung out all night talking about sex, money, and Palestine. Abdallah and I fell asleep on his living room mattress. Another night, we ended up in New Cairo, with Sadhb, the Irish teacher, and a bunch of shady Egyptian boys, the five of us stuffed in a tiny car singing loudly along to The Lonely Island.

"Mai'a! What the fuck is going?" Drew took a swig of beer. "People are trying to convince me that you are a racist. Like, ummm . . . I've known her for over a year. We are good friends and . . ."

His eyes sparkled.

"Yeah, I know, Drew. I don't really understand how everything blew up like that. I wrote a fucking blog post and people are now calling me everything but a child of god." I shook my head and smiled to myself. "Lord, I've written about anti-Blackness in Egypt for three years. And suddenly, I hate white people."

Drew raised an eyebrow. "Yeah, that sounds like bullshit."

"Look, I spent my first year in Cairo hanging out with Sudanese and Ethiopians and, really, mostly with sub-Saharan folks. I lived in Abdeen, the Black neighborhood. And trust me, Black folks talk about the anti-Blackness in Cairo all the time."

"And I know I'm super privileged. I'm American and middle class. Hell, I get way less shit than they do. So when Josh says 'internationals' shouldn't be part of the resistance, because of the way he was treated by a few Egyptians. Shit, some of us have been harassed since the first day we got here."

His black eyebrows twitched. "Plus, the same white girls who are saying you are the racist are constantly complaining about sexual harassment in Cairo."

"Exactly." I lit the cigarette. "By his logic, the only people who should be in Cairo are those who aren't harassed. Okay, if you are white girl and you get harassed, you are an innocent victim. If you are a white boy and you get harassed, you are a hero. If you are a Black girl, you are a self-centered racist. I know Black refugee women who have been super involved in the revolution. Should they leave because they are harassed?

"I fight for this revolution because I want Cairo, this city, this African city, one of the largest and most international in the world, to be a place where bread, freedom, and dignity are available to everyone. To Arabs, to Black Egyptians, to African immigrants, to my daughter, to me. To you. To all of us. I just wanted Josh to think a little deeper about what it meant to be an 'international.' And instead, somehow, me pointing out that white folks feel welcome here got transformed into me being some anti-white, self-centered troll . . ."

He nodded and gave his classic lopsided grin. "Yeah, Mai'a, I get it, I'm Cubano. But I don't think a lot of people think about it like that."

"Obviously, but maybe they should try talking with Black folks here in Cairo. Not even me. Talk to Nubians. Talk to Sudanese. Talk to people who aren't seen as 'international.'" I sighed. "But honestly, I regret writing the fucking post."

Drew grimaced. "I feel you. I don't know why people are going off about this . . ."

"Because people are scared. Cairo became really unpredictable and they don't know how to deal, because for white people Cairo used to feel safe. Trust me, the counterrevolution is going to get a lot worse before it gets better . . . There is a revolution on the streets and folks want to spend their time being haters on me. Okay . . . priorities . . . I'm the Black girl going out to street battles against the police by myself . . ."

"Mai'a, if you want someone to go out with you . . . I'll go . . ."

I grinned and bit my bottom lip. "Thanks, babe. I'll keep that in mind."

"I started reading that Frantz Fanon book you recommended, Mai'a. That Sartre introduction is amazing."

"I was trying to get Josh to read it. I thought it might help. But, of course, now he doesn't even speak to me. Walks out of a room when I walk in." I shrugged. "Whatever . . . That's not what I wanted to talk to you about really." I leaned into the table and it wobbled again. "I want to do this series of salons, like once a month or every two weeks. In my studio, in other people's living rooms. In the summer we could do it on a felucca. And it would bring together poets, visual artists, musicians, intellectuals, journalists, street activists, all together to cross-pollinate and figure out how we want to address the counterrevolution."

"Damn, that sounds awesome . . . Yeah, some people are fucked up. I've heard a couple of girls . . . saying you're crazy. And no one should talk to you." He looked at me apologetically.

I lit another cigarette and inhaled the smoke deep into my lungs and exhaled. "Yet they keep talking about me."

At a New Year's Eve dinner and dance party at Hamed's, who was Sudanese and professional-basketball tall, he greeted us in his rapid-fire English. "My African queens! Welcome! Come in. We are doing African style here. What do you want to drink?"

Mona, my Somali-German friend, who had just flown to Cairo to visit us for a couple of weeks, wearing a loose blue-green floral dress, said, "I'll have a glass of water."

The apartment smelled like peppers and grilled vegetables. The saffron-colored living and dining rooms buzzing with guests and cooks. Hip hop and Afrobeat. A couple of Black Sudanese women in red and purple hijabs giggling in a corner. I waved to them. Rarely at downtown house parties did I see hijabis and even more rarely Black African hijabis. Hamed had brought the downtown scene to the Sudanese-Cairo community. Lovely.

I stood in the hallway by myself, sipping some water and watching people gather. Manu, a skinny, bald Egyptian downtown kid I barely knew, approached me and then, out of nowhere, punched me hard in the jaw.

"You better watch your mouth," he snarled and turned into the kitchen.

I stood there stunned. My jaw throbbing. What the fuck had just happened?

I walked into the bedroom. Mo, who had been a street medic with me during the Muhammad Mahmoud fights, and his girlfriend, Kelly, were sitting on the bed.

"Mai'a, are you okay?"

"That guy Manu just hit me in the jaw . . . I walked over to the corner where the computer was and saw Manu. I barely know him, but I tried to avoid him, because he has made a couple of really creepy comments to me. So I queued my music and walked away. And then he just walked up to me and, like, hit me in the jaw." I burst into tears.

I calmed down, grabbed a can of beer, opened it, walked into the kitchen, said, "Fuck you," and dumped the beer on his head. The foam slid down his face and chest.

Five minutes later, he walked up and poured beer all over me. Hamed and a few other men told him he had to leave. They pushed him outside the apartment and told him to go home.

I was soaked and tired and reeking of alcohol, and we hadn't even had dinner yet. Hamed knelt in front of me, "He can't treat a queen like that."

Michael, the American English teacher who lived in the same apartment building where the downstairs neighbor attacked our party, and a couple other people, had talked to the downstairs Salafi neighbor and said it would be okay for us to have a small going-away party for Mona, my Somali-German friend with almond eyes. The green patio glowed with electric heaters and lamp lights.

Drew, the tall hipster American, had just returned from an academic conference in Berlin and he talked about hanging out in punk bars with Hauke, the German painter who had been arrested as we ran through street fights earlier that spring.

"Mai'a," Drew said. "You would love Berlin."

"Yes! Mai'a, come to Berlin! We can go dancing to hip hop and you can see all the cool places." Mona's large rapt eyes and quick laugh.

"Yeah . . . maybe . . . I just don't like winter or snow, you know. So I'm not sure if Berlin is the place for me right now."

"Just for a quick visit. Just a week or two . . ."

"Maybe . . ."

The Salafi neighbor knocked on the door and demanded that we "end this party now!" Half of our guests left. Abdallah nodded at me, sat down, and folded his arms in front of his chest. And my friends, Drew and his girlfriend, Abdallah and Obada, Sadhb and Meara, stayed calm. Smoking Marlboros, killing time, and laughing at another dramatic night in the city of sin. "God, Mai'a, how do you stay cool about all this?"

Mona left for the airport at about six that morning, and I slept for a few hours. Matt, my ginger-haired New Zealand friend, slept on the couch. Around noon Matt helped me clean up the apartment while talking about race, anarchism, the classic Chomsky vs. Foucault debate, and whales giving birth.

A knock at the door. A petite man with greasy, black hair scowled as I opened it.

"If you ever have Americans or British or French people in this apartment again I will cut your throat! I will kill you!"

"Okay."

"Did you hear me? I will slit your throat!" He pushed me. I held the door against his body and pushed it closed.

I picked up a cigarette off the table and lit it. Matt's mouth hung open.

"How dare he talk to you like that? He would never have spoken to me like that."

"Yes," I said. "You are a tall white guy. Of course he wouldn't talk to you like that."

"And what did he mean about bringing Americans or English people here? You are American!"

"Not in his eyes. In his eyes I'm Sudanese, African, Christian, heathen."

His green eyes looked directly into mine. "But, why aren't you angry . . . angrier?"

I gave a half smile. "This isn't the first guy to threaten my life this week. Sorry, dude, I've run out of energy to care anymore."

What could I say? This was life in Cairo. Violent. On the radio and the television, in conversations in bars, in taxis, on the street, people were angry. Angry at foreigners ruining this country. Angry at foreign women, immodest and drinking alcohol and listening to dirty music and dancing with boys. Angry at Black Africans, uncivilized and corrupting. The rise of the conservative Arab-supremacist Islamists policing the neighborhoods and the foreigners and the Africans and women.

"But yeah, you are right, Matt, I probably should be angry. I probably should feel scared. But I don't. I don't really feel anything at all."

I had arrived in Cairo on January 25, 2009, and lived there for three years, rarely leaving Cairo, never leaving Egypt. I was burnt through, charred and rubble. The price for loving a city of sin and fire.

The next day, I wrote to Mona in Germany. "Hey babe, I'm coming to Berlin in two weeks." I needed to remember what safety felt like.

Mona met me at the airport. Outside fat white flakes fell on my head. I marveled and cursed at the first snow I'd seen in over three years. For the first days, Mona made me breakfast and we listened to jazz while drinking ginger tea with brown sugar.

I barely knew anybody in Berlin and it didn't matter if I did. I walked into bars, cafés, corner stores, and rarely did anyone harass me because I was Black or a woman. I didn't have to justify wanting to spend money in an establishment. I didn't have to fawn and play dumb so people knew I was harmless. I could smile or not smile. Dance in warehouses or just be curious and people watch.

Even though I hated northern winters, it was in the muted days of Berlin, in the quiet of an empty apartment, in the loneliness, with just a cup of coffee and snowdrifts piled on the windows that I regathered the parts of myself I had lost in the depths of Arab street-artist hipsters and rich internationals, fly-in journalists, tear gas, and late-night adventures.

"So, why did you come to Berlin?"

"I'm not sure if you've heard but there's been a revolution for the past year in Egypt and it's gotten really intense. I mean, the night before I left, I went downtown to pick up a few things, and there were protests and the police shooting tear gas and people wearing masks running through the streets and I'm trying to figure out is this in response to the massacre at Port Said, or is it because it is the anniversary of the day when the protesters fought against pro-Mubarak thugs, riding horses and camels, or something else. And I should be scared, at least a little, but I don't feel anything about it. Like, I think I've become too desensitized to the amount of violence I've seen. I just . . . think I should feel something about it."

I sat by myself, in dimly lit cafés, reading books and watching German punks and party kids, Arab and east African, Italian, Spanish, and English folks drink cheap beers and laugh and make out and huddle out of bars into the sunless, grimy mornings. I wrote long passages in my journal and day-dreamed about a simpler life of poetry, mamahood, and sanity.

And I wrote about my father. That summer before, I had finally received his funeral program. And in it, I found another version of my father.

Not the absentee father who lived on the other side of the country and forgot his daughter's birthday and didn't call his children for months and when he did call spent most of the time repeating the same stories about how the world had betrayed him. Not the angry, silent man I had known for most of my life, who had railed against feminists and told me that women weren't as intellectually rigorous as men. But an idealistic young man who had worked with the Black Panthers to create the free breakfast program and child care program in his college, so that single mothers could get an education while their children were safe and fed. A revolutionary who had dedicated his work to mamas and children.

In 2008, while I was in Mexico, I had created a zine called *Revolutionary Motherhood* inspired by the Incite! conference in Denver. Then I had created blogs dedicated to supporting queer, working-class and mothers of color. I had become a doula and a midwife. And now I was working on a book based on the *Revolutionary Motherhood* zine. And I had done all this unbeknownst to me that I was following in a path that my father had walked decades before. I hadn't spoken to him in nearly a decade, but we were blood. I was his legacy. The best of him.

I met Drew and his inky-haired Italian girlfriend, Stefania, at Horreya Café the day after I returned to Cairo.

We talked about mutual friends and Kreuzberg and underground women mc's.

Drew crossed one long leg over the other and leaned in. "Mai'a, are you still selling?"

"Not anymore, darling. I am simplifying my life. And hash just isn't that important to me."

He nodded. "I hear you."

Berlin had given me the miracle I was looking for. The world was mine once again.

A couple of days later, Matt, the redheaded New Zealander who had reminded me to feel something about the violence, called asking if I had hash and invited me to a party happening at the Carlton Hotel bar. Even though I wasn't selling, I wanted to do a favor for Matt, so I called the Egyptian filmmaker Obada to see if he was holding and asked him to meet me at the Carlton. As Matt and I rode a bus downtown, he mentioned it was Josh's going-away party. Fuck.

At the party, I talked with folks and laughed and thought about those times Josh and I had hung out 'til morning. When I said hi to him, he set his thin lips in a line and glared at me for a second and then turned away.

Near the end of the party, I sat in a circle with Matt, an Australian journalist, and Josh. And then a Brown woman with a Western accent whom I had never met sat down in an empty chair next to Josh and started berating me.

"Why did you call Josh a racist?" she folded her arms and huffed.

I looked at Josh and remembered that time we drank two bottles of rosé at Odeon and talked for hours about revolution and anarchism, gender and race, street artists and hip hop, Occupy and decolonization.

"I didn't call him a racist."

"Yes, you did," she growled. "I read the fucking blog post."

"Yeah, and I didn't—"

She jabs her finger in the air toward me. "Yeah but you were implying that he was a racist."

"Actually, I wasn't. I was saying that Blackness—"

She snapped, "Why did you even bring race into it? His writing isn't about race! I know Josh! He is not a racist."

"Okay, but actually—"

"Josh is a really nice guy! Why did you even come here?"

I looked over at Matt, who had invited me to this party. Matt stared blankly at the wall. The Australian journalist snickered.

"Wow." My eyes were hot and I didn't want to cry in front of them. "Fuck this. I'm going back to Berlin."

I walked off to the bathroom. When I returned, they were leaving. I sat down and stared off at the open sky. There were no stars in the sky. Light pollution, smog, a city fearful of Blackness. I couldn't stop crying.

A waitress softly handed me a napkin and asked if I wanted another drink. I was sure I could hear an old Gil Scott-Heron song far in the deep black night. I was sure I heard an old church hymn, a call to altar. I fingered the plastic bead necklace Aza made for me before I left for Berlin.

Drummond, my loud, witty, Scottish, drunk friend, called me up Tuesday evening. He was in town and there was someone he wanted me to meet. Perfect. We chatted under the blue and black lights of Cairo Jazz Club. His new girl-friend, with long, light hair and sweet eyes, was clearly in love. Ebullient, he bought candied cocktails and outlined his plans to move to Thailand with her.

"What do you think?" he asked.

"She's perfect for you."

"I know she's fifteen years younger than me, but . . ."

"Yeah, but I like her. I really like her."

He grinned. He couldn't stop grinning.

I hugged both of them goodbye and took a taxi home early. I hadn't slept much the night before.

When the driver stopped the car on my street, he demanded triple the usual fee. We argued. I gave him the normal amount plus baksheesh.

"This is the normal price. I know it. You knew it. Every taxi driver in Cairo knew that."

I walked out of the taxi. This is how I often handled taxi drivers who demanded exorbitant prices.

Behind me, the taxi driver was yelling incoherently. I heard his voice getting closer. He grabbed my shoulder and tried to wrestle the purse out of my hand. All I can remember is him punching me in the right shoulder again. Him screeching that I was Black and a whore.

Around us the street was somber, the stores gated and shuttered. Except for the white glare from a late-night smoothie shop half a block away, the world was asleep. A cracking sound in my shoulder girdle and then numbness. I ran to my apartment building and slammed the door. The elderly bowab peeped out from his bed under the stairs.

"That man wants to hit me." I said pointing to the door. Then I ran upstairs to my apartment.

In the morning I awoke weeping in pain. Cal bought me a white sling from the medical supply store, which I wore for next few days. I could barely touch my right arm without searing pain.

I bought plane tickets back to Berlin.

I visited Drew and Stefania, his raven-haired girlfriend, in their apartment that evening. We listened to emerging female hip hop. I told them everything that had happened in the past couple of days: Josh's party, the taxi driver, why I was wearing a sling, my decision to return to Berlin.

"Damn, Mai'a. Damn."

"Yeah, the weirdest part is that I don't even know who that chick is. I didn't want to get in some argument with some Brown chick in front of three white guys over whether or not that white guy is a racist. Like, that just seemed so wrong . . . but I have never met her and she's acting like I owe her an explanation."

Drew winced, "Well, Mai'a . . . I think I know who she is."

"Drew?" I raised an eyebrow. "Who the fuck is she?"

He took a deep breath and rubbed his fingers through his curls. "Sara. She is at AUC and was in Berlin with me for the conference last month . . . One night Hauke and I and Sara went out for drinks. And she's talking about this girl Mai'a and how she wrote this blog post and how she's the 'real racist' and you hate white people . . . and then Hauke and I look at each other and we burst out laughing. And we can't stop laughing, and so we finally tell her that yeah, we know you. I'm really good friends with you, and you and Hauke are friends, and we know you really well, and yeah, you aren't racist against white people."

I shake my head. "Really . . . What the fuck do people expect when they write a blog? That no one is going to respond? He posted the thing on Facebook. Who starts a blog about anarchist politics and the Arab Spring and then acts like a hurt dog when someone responds to it? Why have a blog if you don't expect for folks to be in conversation with what you post? People attack me, personal attacks, against me, against my kid, on my blogs. And I'm expected to just take it, because you know, it's the internet. It's social media, whatever. But he gets one, frankly, well-argued critique and he acts like I told him to go commit suicide. Lord, but you know what, I didn't even call Josh a racist. But now, I do think he is a racist. Really. Because if you really think that the Black experience is irrelevant in African revolutions. Then yeah, you're an intellectual racist."

The night before I left for Berlin, Aza and I cut up an old dress of mine, draped it and hand-sewed a little blue and green floral dress with cap sleeves and a long full skirt for her. These six weeks would be the longest we had ever been apart. "I'll be back soon. Soon, baby girl, soon." We snuggled in bed together, her regaling me with rambling fairy tales with no endings. I promised her I would be back for her birthday for the five-year-old princess tea party in mid-April.

Neukölln. Kreuzberg. Friedrichshain. Parks and local celebrations. Paper collage and spray paint, middle-class kids marching against gentrification, and low-cost Turkish bakeries. I rented an apartment in Neukölln and rode my bike every day along the river that early spring. The air of the city, clear silence, stillness, and light.

I sat in funky, hipster, punk cafés, lit by lily-white taper candles. Salsa music spilling from the speakers. Grungy boys and rude girls snarling in German and drinking, their faces weathered from the cold. Tall bones shining through the translucent skin. Dressed in dark, neutral colors, decorated in studied carelessness. The unkemptness of the well-to-do. Staring into lit screens, Apple laptops and iPhones. Older women, with ivory hair, reading newspapers. Two-euro pints at the demon's hour. I watched them, learning again how not to give a fuck.

I returned to Cairo five days before Aza's birthday. To that desert city I loved so much, to that revolution I still wanted to believe in.

Paper Dreams

A gust of wind slammed against me, the air gritty, dark mandarin, blinding. I struggled against the wind, battled to open the back door of the taxi that had swerved on the sidewalk and stopped in front me. I tumbled into the backseat, my mouth full of sharp, tiny slivers.

"El khamseen," the driver said to me.

"Na'am." I'd forgotten that every spring came the fifty days of sandstorms in Cairo.

On the radio, the newscaster talked politics. The first legitimate election for an Egyptian president was finally happening.

For months leading up to the election, the city buzzed. Campaign posters scattered the streets. The two main candidates, Muhammad Morsi and Ahmed Shafik, were both horrible. Morsi was a leader of the Muslim Brotherhood. The Brotherhood had promised during the parliamentary elections that they would not run a presidential candidate, thus making it safe for Egyptians to vote for the Muslim Brotherhood to run the parliament. Then the Brotherhood broke their promise. Shafik had served as the last prime minister under Mubarak. There was a new revolutionary law saying that those from the old regime couldn't take political office in the new government, but the courts made an exception for Shafik.

The redheaded New Zealander, Matt, held a house party in his apartment in Governorate Giza. The ancient pyramids glowed electric blue and gold at night, and his rooftop had the perfect view. Our Egyptians friends talked about the election. Most of them were going to abstain from voting.

"Who are we supposed to vote for? The choice is between the military and the mosque. This is not what our friends died for. We marched and fought and mourned and made art for us. We laughed through the nights when it was too dark to go outside. We became something more than just our individual visions of freedom. We put ourselves, our families, our hope on the line for a better Egypt, but we are constantly pushed aside for the mosques, and the military, the Brotherhood, and the old guard. The revolution doesn't matter. It failed. We are tired of this mess and heartbroken."

"No," I shook my head. "We are the revolution—and it fails when we do. And we fail when we give up." A couple of guys murmured in assent, but most, I could tell, didn't want to hear about a dying dream.

In mid-June Egyptians went to the ballot box. For a week and a half, the country waited while the electoral commission recounted every vote, while the military and Mubarak's old guard, businessmen, and Islamist leaders huddled in smoky back rooms choosing the president. Political gossip engulfed the city. Finally, it was announced that Morsi, the Muslim Brotherhood candidate, had won by two percentage points. Shafik, his opponent, fled the country, claiming that the results were false. Gossip said that Morsi had won because the military was afraid of more street rebellions.

Cal, Aza, and I moved from Cairo to Dahab, a Bedouin, eco-tourist beach town in South Sinai. A modicum of peace. We sat on a rooftop Thai restaurant at sunset overlooking the Red Sea. Vermilions, peaches, indigos brushing across the sky. The sun hidden by a swath of clouds. Empty bowls on the table that once held sweet and spicy pad thai and green curry with shrimp. A couple of bottles of wine half empty. Sadhb, the pixie Irish girl from Cairo, and Dylan, a ruddy-faced Welsh guy, chatted with us languidly. Sadhb and Dylan had come from the city to the beach for a long weekend.

"Hey, Mai'a, remember him?" Dylan flipped his phone to me. I squinted my eyes. A photo of Manu.

"Well, you do have violent friends."

"What? This is Manu. Remember him?"

"Yeah, Manu, the guy who attacked me twice. Yeah, I remember him. Goes by 'Manu Chao' on Facebook. The guy who punched me in my chin on New Year's Eve. And then punched me in the back of the head last summer."

Dylan's jaw dropped. "That's not possible . . . He's gay."

I started laughing. The sun dropped below the clouds and rested on the indigo mountains in the far-off horizon.

"Mai'a, what happened?" Sadhb asked.

I told them about Hamed's New Year's Eve party.

She narrowed her eyes. "Manu was just crying to me about how hard his life was because he's Egyptian and gay . . ."

I took a long sip of the pale-yellow wine, held it up to the horizon, and watched the sun stretch and shimmer in the glass. "And then in July, I was at this house party on the roof, and Dylan, you came up to me. And I remember asking you, 'Oh god, is Manu here?' Because I knew you two hung together. And you were like 'yeah . . .' A few minutes later I was looking over the roof, my back turned to the party. And out of nowhere I felt this punch in the back of my head and I fell forward. Thankfully my arm caught my fall. It scraped on the concrete ledge. See, here?" I stood out of my chair, lifted my wrist and showed Dylan the two-inch dark scar that cut down my wrist. "I mean, the ledge wasn't that high, what if I had fallen off?"

"Woah." He grabbed my wrist and stared at it.

I shook my hand away. "So, anyways, I turned around, walked up to him. And then the host, this chick who I didn't know, grabbed my arm and pulled me out of the party. The whole time I'm like, 'What the fuck? That guy just attacked me.'"

"But why would he do that? He's gay, Mai'a."

Aza leaned against my calf under the restaurant table, playing with her stuffed animal. I reached down and ran my fingers through her soft hair.

"I don't know him. I met him and instantly thought he was . . . off. This one time at like 3:00 a.m., he started sending these creepy Faccbook messages. I asked him to stop and he wouldn't. So, finally I blocked him. A couple of months later he punched me in the chin.

"Anytime after that when I saw him at a party or even at Horreya, he'd be staring me down, following me around the room. It was fucking crazy. I started carrying a knife. Once he was stalking me at this party, and so I just got tired of it and started following him slowly instead. I was tired of being scared all the time. This girl, Miriam, who was visiting from Berlin, noticed that something was wrong and asked me about it. And she was shocked that people were still letting him hang out, so she started stalking him with me. He started screaming, claiming that I was trying to kill him. Even though I was just following him around the party like he had been doing to me for months. People were freaking out and trying to push me away even though I was feet away from him at all times. Finally, he left.

"A couple of months later, he punched me the second time. He was living in my neighborhood in Doqqi and I was afraid of what he'd do if I saw him on the streets. I was afraid for Aza. That's why I moved to Garden City and stayed with our friend, Mandolin. That's why I'm not in Cairo anymore."

Dylan pulled his phone out. "I'm going to call him. I'm going to call him right now."

"That's not really necessary, dude."

I turned back to the sea. I loved these last moments before the sun disappeared and the air became dusk. It was ablaze, like a street fire, like a Bloody Mary.

"Hello? Manu?" Dylan glances up at me. "I'm sitting here in Dahab with Mai'a. And she told me that you've punched her twice? . . . I mean, she just showed me this bruise and it's pretty nasty . . . Okay, but did you hit her? Like, I need to know . . . Hello? Manu? Manu!?"

He looked at his phone. "He hung up."

Dylan rang again. No answer.

I turned to Sadhb. "I think that proves my point."

"But why?" Dylan peered at his phone as if it could answer.

"I don't know what he has against me other than the fact that I didn't want to hang out with him. I always thought he was creepy and then he proved it by attacking and stalking me. So . . . yeah . . . I trust my instincts."

A silhouette of birds with large wingspans cut across the sky. The sea's soft drone. The red, red sun floating down to earth.

"Did you tell anyone?" He looked over at Cal who had been silent this whole time. Cal said nothing.

"I told everyone, dude. And, it doesn't matter. If Drew or Matt were hosting the party, they wouldn't let him in. But other folks didn't really seem to care or to believe me. One person said, 'Oh well, you know, that's just the way this scene is . . .' Honestly, I barely knew Miriam but she got it. But most people . . ." I shook my head.

"Fuck."

We sat in silence. "Watch," I said. "The last moments are . . ." And there it was, that dying heart, that roar of color and light, one more day falling into darkness. We sat there watching a sky that was always evolving, finding new ways to throw blush and hues on the world.

"Hey let's go out tonight and have a good time and forget about all this Manu stuff . . ." Dylan stuffed his phone back in his pocket.

I didn't want to go out, but I didn't want to go home either. I wanted to sit by the beach at night and listen to the waves. But every time I tried to do that, some Egyptian or Bedouin boy would insist on sitting with me "for my protection" and then start hitting on me.

I just wanted to live in paradise and be free and safe at night. Maybe in my next lifetime.

Six months later, spring 2013, I heard violence coming like a rumble in the distance. Fear nested in my bones. I couldn't wash it away with a saltwater swim. Or with a few late-night beers and a good conversation.

Cal had moved back to the United States for work in the beginning of 2013. Over the past year, after graduating from AUC with a degree in international law, he fell into a mute depression. We had agreed for years that after AUC, he would get an NGO job, preferably in Africa. Instead, he sat on his couch and bed, drinking clear bottles of cheap liquor, refusing to speak or do more than the bare daily minimum in life. While the rest of his classmates found work in international NGOs or entered doctoral programs, he seemed to be an immobile boulder, empty eyes. Then in late autumn of 2012, he announced he was returning to the United States to live with his parents in Minnesota and find work there. I said, "Okay." What more could I do? Honestly, I was angry at trying to decipher his wordless lies by omission, of trying to build a life with someone who was an inarticulate cocoon.

We had always been fairly independent, connected by our deep commitment to social change, shared books and our love for Aza. But now he was a phantasm, blowing away to the United States with a few pairs of pants and some T-shirts.

It was Aza and me left in a one-bedroom apartment, filled with four years of books, clothes, furniture, posters, and toys. A five-minute walk from the Red Sea. An eight-hour drive from Cairo.

In Dahab, there was no revolution or street battles. No armored tanks. No street art celebrating the martyrs. Just vacationers and divers. Just businesses trying to make another pound.

The Red Sea, so clear and blue, we tiptoed into the water and marveled at the bottle-green fish swimming around our feet. Cheap bars, with 2:00 a.m. last call and cheap weed growing wild on the mountains.

Aza scampered on the beach in clunky beach shoes and worn sweaters, her curly hair matted from the salty sea water. I read books, made small talk with foreigners and Bedouins, and followed the daily news online. I finished writing projects on my silver laptop at a seaside café, while Aza swam in the late afternoons.

But to travel the eight-hour ride from Dahab to Cairo, by car or bus, meant we had to pass through the long stretch of the Sinai. Every time we took the trip, army checkpoints and police checkpoints and stories of foreigners being kidnapped and held for ransom, blossomed. State security imprisoned and tortured sub-Saharan refugees who crossed the Sinai desert into Israel without papers.

Arab Egyptians often mistook me for Sudanese or Nigerian. It was the U.S. passport and my light-skinned daughter that convinced soldiers and police to let me safely pass. But every time we journeyed across the Sinai, I was taking a larger and larger risk.

The energy and sound, the light of Cairo transformed. The optimism and hope of the heady days of the revolution evaporated as the city grew more conservative. Kids still hung out in downtown Cairo, and its surrounding neighborhoods, Zamalek, Doqqi, Mohandeseen. There'd still be homemade grenades bursting open with fire and light and activists taking over the streets, but I couldn't tell who was on whose side anymore. Splinter groups proliferated among the activists. I started asking our friends: What is the difference between a revolution and a civil war? My old haunting grounds had begun to smell like war.

When Aza and I stayed in Cairo we shared an apartment with our friend Aisha, Sam's now ex-wife, and her three-year-old son, Bikar. Aza and Bikar looked like they were siblings, sienna coils of hair falling into their dark almond eyes.

Aisha and her son lived in an apartment in Giza, which was technically a separate governante from Cairo, but everyone treated Giza like it was just one more sprawling working-class Cairene neighborhood.

I had been Aisha's midwife in the fall of 2010. A water birth in a plastic kiddie pool. Bob Marley and Fairouz crooning from the laptop speakers. Wax candles burning on the wooden shelves. Sam rocking with her through the painful hours. Me reading a book in the corner or breathing and moaning with her. Around 1:00 a.m., her labor stalled.

Abdallah, her brother, had promised to assist the birth, but every time I called, he was still at Horreya with Obada.

I called him again.

"Abdallah you need to come."

"Mashi."

"No really Abdallah, get in a taxi and come. I'll pay for it. She needs you here."

"Mai'a, it's not important," he moaned.

"It's life, Abdallah. It's as important as life."

Bikar was born in warm water, in the blood and the caul, near the Giza pyramids, less than an hour after Abdallah stepped into the room.

"You see, Abdallah, he was waiting for you."

Sam rode me to my apartment later that morning. Cairo was waking up. Freshly baked bread piled high on wooden cartons. Children in faded, ultramarine school uniforms walking down the sidewalks. Large trucks pumping diesel exhaust into the teeming streets. He parked in front of the building and looked at me like he didn't know what to do. I hugged him, "You are going to be a great father. Really. Go home and take care of your wife, so your wife can take of your baby."

Two and a half years later, when Aza and I rode taxis from Giza to downtown Cairo, too often the, taxi drivers would yell at me, at us, demanding more money than we had agreed, calling the police to force us to pay them.

"Mama, I hope the taxi driver isn't mean this time," Aza said as a black-and-white taxi stopped for us.

I rubbed my fingers through her curls. "I know, m'ija, don't worry."

Still, Aza's hands shook while I negotiated the price with the drivers.

One warm spring night in Giza, I was reclining on a mattress in the olive living room, having survived another taxi ride. Aza slept next to me, but my wired nerves kept me awake.

Social scientists report that summer was when violence peaked globally. Hot days mixed with boredom and it all boiled into the streets. I had spent the past few summers celebrating Ramadan, while enduring thirsty boys hanging off cars in the afternoon, waiting to breakfast. I walked the city, avoiding the street fights and harassment that erupted like flames from dry kindling.

Why was I staying in Egypt?

Because I was afraid to leave the only home we knew. But war was coming and I didn't know what surviving that would do to us.

I decided to go to Berlin. One summer of peace. And maybe in the fall I'd return to Egypt and fall back in love with it. Maybe the summer in Egypt would be quiet and I'd feel foolish having run away.

I felt guilty. Aisha couldn't leave Egypt, neither could her son, Bikar, or most of my Egyptian and Palestinian friends. But Aza and I could.

I was crossing Talaat Harb Square, when a motorbike zipped in front of me and circled back.

"Sam!"

He always had a magical way of showing up when I needed him.

"Mai'a! Habibti. You going to Horreya?"

"Yes."

"Get on. I'll take you."

He whipped through the streets and parked in front of the café.

Milad placed two beers on our table. I picked at the green-and-white Stella logo peeling off the table top.

"Where's Aza?" Sam asked

"She's with my mom at the hotel." My mother was visiting us in Cairo for the first time.

I held up my beer bottle, "Cheers! This is my last night in Cairo."

"No. Mai'a. Where are you going?"

"To Berlin."

Sam groaned, "You should stay here. You belong here."

I shook my head, "I don't think so. I love Cairo, but I don't think it loves me."

We talked about Aisha and Bikar and the last months they were together. "It was horrible, Mai'a." His eyes bored into me. "I know you think I did mean things to her. But . . ."

He was right. Three years ago, when I was Aisha's midwife, I had been very protective of her. When they had a fight, I tried to take care of both of them, but especially her, because she was a woman, because she was nine months pregnant.

We walked into Odeon and were greeted by a table of a dozen people singing the songs of Umm Kulthum and other classic Egyptian songs. We joined them and laughed. I sang along even though I didn't know the words.

"I need to marry someone like you or Tilde."

"I like Tilde." Tilde was the blond Belgium woman he was seeing. She was sweet and smart and stood her ground.

He pulled out his DSLR camera and took pictures of me. "Marry me!"

"No. I make a horrible wife."

"Not for me you wouldn't."

"Trust me. I'm too independent."

"Well, then at least kiss me."

I laughed. "No."

We didn't leave the hotel bar until after the sunlight broke the horizon.

The sandy sunlight in spring. He parked in front of my hotel. I ran upstairs to grab some cash. When I went back to the street, he was gone. I waited for twenty minutes. Called his phone several times, but no answer.

Shit. The police had probably arrested him again.

Sam was flaky, but he wouldn't just leave like that and not return.

He called me a couple of days later. The police had finally released him.

The first weeks in Berlin, it rained daily. In the afternoons, we watched the cold waters slam against the windows. In our tiny hotel room, Aza and I had two suitcases, one broken laptop, two fairy books and four plastic bags of damp clothes because I couldn't figure out how to make the dryer work at the waschhaus.

I was trying to grow a life out of the detritus of our ship-wrecked past in Egypt.

Everything was new to us in that country. I spoke no German except for pleasantries: guten tag, bitte, danke, auf wiedersehen. I did most of our shopping errands at the Lebanese-owned stores using my hodgepodge Egyptian/Palestinian Arabic. The German language sounded cold, and I missed the desert sounds and spices. At nights, I drank wine with spritzer, listened to sad songs and wrote about freedom and love and revolution and the Middle East and Africa and mothering and exile.

i tell her that fairies are real, but i'm not sure about god.

she tells me that god lives inside of her. somewhere near her heart. and that everyone has their own god. that my god made her god and her god made her.

that when you die, you go into the earth. and become part of the dirt, the earth, the flowers and the trees. the plants that we eat.

and when i explained to her that the huge poster, in our living room, of bob marley exhaling a spliff, that bob marley is dead. she told me that bob marley is part of the plants and trees that we eat, and then exclaimed, we eat bob marley's head!

she says she believes in fairies and aliens, even though she has never seen them, because the universe is really big and she hasn't seen most of it. she points to the world map that hangs upside down in her father's room and shows me all the countries she has never been to, but still believes they exist.

she draws pictures of mermaids and wonders if she will ever see one when she is swimming in the sea.

she wants me to explain everything to her. how clouds make rain. and why it doesn't snow in egypt. and who will she be when she grows up. what does it feel like to be a bird and why sometimes there isn't money in our bank account. why her father had to leave to go to america. and why am i sad some days. and why her friends say mean things about her and what is the wind saying at night. why i get mad when i see a blond girl in a headdress at the parade and why do the teachers not let the kids play, but instead make them sit in their chairs and listen to the teacher.

i don't know why fire can hurt people and so can water,
but there are firefighters but not water fighters.

why america is so far away and egyptians call her white,
but in america, people call her brown.

why people think kids shouldn't be in smoky bars, but
dogs can be.

i don't know why everyone can't see that the cascades of
curly brown is beautiful, but straight yellow hair is.

of course boys can wear dresses, but the girls are usually
stronger.

of course love is more important than money.

of course, baby, people are silly. and have silly ideas. and
you are too smart for all that.

We learned it was important in Germany to follow the rules exactly, wait our turns in line, always be five minutes early, carry rain gear no matter how sunny it was when you strolled out the door. I watched Berliners' body language and clothing choices and translated for Aza. Sometimes I even got it right.

"Here," I gestured to a middle-aged couple stiff-backed and frowning in an underground Metro station, "people whisper their disagreements. They don't want to yell in public."

"Why not?" Aza asked.

"They are embarrassed to show their emotions to other people."

Surrounded by a faint urine scent, she and I told inside jokes about our Cairo friends and recited Nicki Minaj's "Beez in the Trap" while we waited for the next subway train.

I knelt on the floor of the bright yellow living room of my Berlin apartment, my laptop reposed on my mattress, and cried. Aza was in her messy, sage-green bedroom, with scissors and scotch tape, making paper houses and paper dreams, as I watched all our dreams of revolution burn up and blow apart.

A month before, in July, the Egyptian army had removed the newly elected president, Muhammad Morsi, in response to millions of people protesting in the streets for days demanding his ouster.

Once again, I wrote, the people have demanded a recall vote from the streets.

When he was deposed, the supporters of Morsi and the Muslim Brotherhood staged a series of sit-ins protesting the removal of the president. The largest of which was at Raba'a Mosque. One afternoon I woke up to the news that Egyptian state forces had attacked Raba'a and the death toll was already at a couple of hundred in just a few hours.

My German landlord and I hung out that evening. He tried to distract me from my laptop. Telling cute stories about his job and his daughter and some anti-nuclear protest that he'd participated in a couple of years ago in Germany.

He'd never been to Egypt. Never marched in Cairo with a million people. Never spent nights dreaming a revolution that sparked uprisings all over the Arab world. His friends weren't messaging him, scared to leave their apartments or even worse, having lost their housing and trying to figure out where they could possibly rest for more than just a night.

Cute stories were the last thing I wanted.

"Well, at least you are here," he said. "You are safe."

As I watched the footage from Raba'a, I kept repeating, "They didn't have to do it. Why? Why did they do this?" The military government, days before, had announced plans to disperse the activists of Raba'a in three stages over the next three months, nonviolently. Then days later, the security forces slaughtered them.

If we'd stayed in Cairo, would I have been in Raba'a, in a white scarf, a long-sleeved button-down shirt and long skirt? Even if I didn't support the Muslim Brotherhood, would I have slipped on a hijab and backpack and documented it all? Would I have survived the massacre?

I put Aza to bed. In the morning, I'd tell her what had happened.

I fell asleep with my face caked in salt water and dreamt of fire.

After Raba'a, most folks stopped fighting for the revolution. Abdel Fattah El-Sisi, the Minister of Defense, called curfew on the city. And kids stayed home. They watched movies on satellite TV and played card games and drank rich coffee and stopped looking out their windows. During the 2011 revolution, the army had called a curfew and people defied it every night, claiming their right to free movement in Tahrir Square. The only people now willing to fight in the streets were the Muslim Brotherhood, who had lost their president, their government, and their comrades. It was summer and the war had come.

When the army removed Mubarak from office two years before, it was clear to many that it was done under the orders of the United States. I listened to so many arguments about whether this was a revolution or a coup. The Egyptian army, which controlled 25–40 percent of the economy, took control of the country before truly losing control. While some folks uncritically cheered the army, intoning that "the army and the people are one hand," others said that for the revolution to be fulfilled, the military government would have to be taken out of power, so that a true civilian government could emerge. There were always rumors and reports of the revolution being financed and orchestrated by outside forces, Americans, Europeans, the Gulf states, traitors and factions from within the government who wanted Mubarak gone. Cairo ran on rumors, intrigue, and drama. It was the capital of the Arab film world.

In the days after Raba'a, my Cairo friends messaged me with more and more stories. State security knocking on doors looking for dissidents, for Muslim brothers, for Morsi supporters, for gay men and activists. All of them.

After the military government took over, security forces hunted thousands of Muslim brothers in the streets. Imprisoned thousands and gave life sentences for the crime of supporting Morsi, supporting the results of an election a year ago. Or supporting freedom of speech. Or for walking outside after dark.

I hadn't supported Morsi. I didn't support El Sisi, the new, de facto Egyptian leader. I didn't support the dreams of affluent Egyptian kids who fantasized turning Egypt into a wannabe European country. I didn't support the Muslim Brotherhood's dreams of making the country even more conservative, even more intolerant of differences and freedom. I supported the kids in the streets fighting for a better life, the kids with Molotov cocktails and slingshots, the kids who fought on the front lines for freedom.

Morsi was pushed out of office and the army took over again. It looked like the same script and it was. Except this time the army was much more brutal. This time the police weren't kicked out of the city but given free rein. This time El-Sisi was taking prisoners by the hundreds.

The army had learned their lesson from two years ago: terrorize the city into submission. And it worked.

In early October, Aza and I flew back to Egypt for six weeks, to pack up our stuff from our apartment. We stayed in Aurora's apartment in the Cairene neighborhood, Mohandiseen. When we went to Horreya, Milad cheered, "Mai'a! Aza!" He brought me a beer and her a nonalcoholic malt drink.

Aza covered her ears and scrunched up her face, "Why is it so loud?"

"Berlin spoiled us. We have to get used to the noise again."

The noise had never bothered me before, but now all of downtown was deafening.

October 6th was an Egyptian national holiday celebrating the Yom Kippur War. We rode with Sam that evening to the 6th of October Bridge and climbed up a tower. We perched like birds and blew up balloons and threw them off the bridge, watching them fall to the Nile waters and then float away.

We perched like birds watching the balloons and boats float beneath us.

In the distance on my right, I saw two figures approaching us. I turned and made eye contact with Sam a few inches behind me.

"I see them," he said.

When they got closer to us, Sam hopped onto his feet. Their postures were menacing. I could only hear pieces of their conversations. I saw the glint of a knife. My heart shivered, but I knew Sam had always tried to protect Aza and me.

I spoke softly to Aza, "Hey, look at that boat with all the lights on it. I wonder if it is a wedding party . . . Oh, and see that one over there? The felucca with the white sail?"

My heart shivered. I didn't like those boys and I didn't like how long Sam was gone talking to them.

Sam returned with the two boys. Greasy dark hair and thick black T-shirts.

"Hey, so these guys want to meet you and Aza. They wanted to know where you are from. I told them America."

"Who are these guys?"

"They are from Ain Shams." He chuckled, "I told them I am from Ain Shams, but they didn't believe me."

"Why not."

"Because I'm with you. And you are Black . . . Then they wanted to take my motorbike. They told me to give them the keys."

"I was afraid of that."

"But everything's okay now."

I shook the boys' hands and we exchanged salaams.

Sam and they talked a bit more. I held onto Aza, trying to follow the conversation.

Finally, they left. Sam sat back down. A long exhale, like a balloon deflating.

Our last day in Cairo, the city was preparing for the second anniversary of Muhammad Mahmoud. Aza and I toured the street art on the walls and I told her the stories from two years ago when the streets had been alive with fire and hope.

We turned the corner. Now, the street was lined with large black tanks.

"Should we go this way?" I wanted to see what the military had planned for the protesters.

"No, Mama, we shouldn't go that way. That looks scary."

This was the first time I remembered Aza being scared of military tanks. I stared at the soldier on top of the closest armored vehicle for a moment. I remembered the nights in January 2011 when we danced on top of tanks and soldiers high-fived the revolutionaries amidst the street fires and broken Molotov cocktails.

Aza was probably right. Those tanks did look scary. We turned and walked back to our hotel.

On our last night, Aza and I had sat with Sam and Tilde and Aurora in one of the outdoor coffee shops downtown. Curfew had finally been lifted after months, and it was past midnight on a Thursday night and downtown Cairo was alive once again. The coffee shops were overflowing with people, motorbikes parked on the sidewalks. Sam's girlfriend, Tilde, was pregnant and Sam was overjoyed.

As the plane ascended, I looked over the dirty and ancient city, bursting with twenty million people.

For all the violence. The strange ways that we congregated and made love and made war and made mistakes. For the soft nights and the harsh days. For the Nile, the river Styx, the waters that run forever. For us running and running and running toward the daylight. For the nights. Always always for the nights. For forever. For yesterday. For that last night and this daybreak that makes the sky screams like heaven itself is on fire.

For tomorrow. For children. For the heart of the sun. For forever. I will not forget. I will not remember you like a sepia photograph held in front of the camera. I will not pretend like it didn't matter because we didn't win. Yet. Or maybe ever. Even still I will remember. For a minute. For a month. For a year. For a breath. We believed in freedom. And we believed we could challenge power. And we believed we could win.

I've seen the fading embers. The horrid faces contorting into madness and sainthood. And I said yes. And so did you. And if you didn't you were the fool. Because when will you ever live like that again. When will you ever believe in a people and a dance and shaabi music and the streets running wet and hungry.

If you refuse to believe. you don't know what human is.

Because for a minute we were alive like a wail flying down the dry streets. And it was winter, not spring. And it was Africa. Our skin glittering black. And the mother of life was no longer just a vacation spot. Or a place to wait for the U.S. State Department to say, "Another people well trained." No, we were alive like the bark of wild dogs and a fist tapping out a poem on the edge of parchment and bloody skin.

Sign my name.

Sign my name again.

I will not say I have no regrets. I regret not loving freedom harder.

I regret that I believed that those leisure-suited men had hearts that turned toward justice like tortured prisoners turn toward the sun.

I do not regret loving freedom and fighting for us. Fighting for myself. I do not regret fighting for my daughter.

I do not regret the songs I heard in the streets and sidewalks of a madcap city.

I do not regret our revolution

Sign my name on that paper dream. Sign my name again.

This Is How We Survive

Cornfields and wind turbines, meadowed cows, and hay bales. The sun setting in the rear window of Cal's rusted silver minivan. NPR and pop music radio stations drone on. Cal was driving Aza and me two and a half hours to south Minneapolis.

Bev, a white, single mama in Minneapolis, messaged me in early October, asking if I wanted to go with her to Standing Rock. Our kids had fall break and she and her Iraqi-American son, Isa, were returning to Standing Rock for a few days.

I had followed the struggle in Standing Rock between the Indigenous-led water protectors and the North Dakota police for the past few months online. The Lakota Sioux nation had been fighting to stop Dakota Access Pipeline (DAPL) from being built. Energy Transfer Partners (ETP), the owner of DAPL, was trying to build an oil pipeline underneath the Missouri River, one of the main waterways in the United States. An oil spill would threaten the water supply of up to eighteen million people. Furthermore, ETP planned to build the pipeline on the Lakota Sioux's treaty land. The 1851 Treaty of Fort Laramie between the U.S. government and the Lakota nation recognized that the land belonged to the Sioux nation. The Army Corps of Engineers had tried to buy the land from the Lakota, but they had refused to cede it. The Lakota youth began the resistance against the pipeline.

After months of resistance, national and international media had started paying attention to Standing Rock. More than two hundred Native nations and tribes had come to stand with the Lakota against DAPL, which Native folk called the "black snake" from prophecy.

My family was from northern South Carolina and was Indigenous and Black. My mother's maiden name, Lowery, was the same last name that was the most common last name in the Native tribe the closest to my family's hundred-acre homestead. As a child, I had learned through research that during the Civil War, the Lowerys had been a maroon, guerrilla, multiracial, Native group that had attacked Confederate whites in North and South Carolina. After the war, North Carolina offered the Lowerys' status as "Indians," which would be a higher status than Blacks, but lower than whites, in an effort to discourage them organizing with Blacks in the region. They later started calling themselves "Lumbee Indians." My family were identified as Black on public records, no matter their skin tone. But we were Native, too, and we never forgot that.

Aza and I had moved into Cal's house in a small, white, conservative Minnesota town about a year and a half ago. I had decided to bring Aza to Winona because Cal was too psychologically weak to live anywhere away from his parents or to work anywhere but at the mindless factory job he had gotten in the town. She needed a stronger relationship with her father, and I knew how hard it was to grow up being unsure if your father cared about you. Winona, Minnesota. Population: 97 percent white. Famous for bluffs, stained glass, and the Mississippi River that ran through it.

I borrowed camping supplies from Cal's parents and from a coworker of Cal's. Flashlights and water bottles, a four-person tent, and cold weather sleeping bags littered the dining room the days before we were leaving. We bought winter pants and sweaters at the local Goodwill and thick socks, hand warmers, lighters, and snacks at the dollar store.

Aza piped up from the backseat, "You know, Mama, the only people I hate are Donald Trump and Justin Bieber."

I laughed, "I can understand that." I looked out the window at the farmhouses and gray grasses and asked Cal, "What is the difference between bluffs and hills?"

Cal checked the GPS and said, "Bluffs are hills next to rivers."

"That's it? I never get why Winona folks are constantly lauding their 'bluffs.' Like are they just hills?" I chuckled, "That's horrible."

Aza piped up. "Can we change the radio?"

"Sure. Is this a Justin Bieber song?"

"Yes. And he is so annoying!"

We arrived to a large house in south Minneapolis. Bev, a tall woman with red hair, answered the door.

The next day the four of us piled into a car Bev had borrowed. My license expired after spending nearly seven years outside of the United States, so Bev drove the entire way. Isa, her thirteen-year-old son, anxiously checked his reflection to make sure his hair was on point. Aza, bundled up in a rose and white lined hoodie, her head buried in a book.

While riding shotgun, I looked at my phone's map and exclaimed, "Oh my god. I just realized that North Dakota is right next to Minnesota."

Bev who had grown up in Minnesota laughed, "What are you talking about?"

"I had no idea where North Dakota was. Ask me where Tunisia is or Peru on a map, I could tell you. But when I was in high school, we used to have this joke, that North Dakota was a CIA invention . . ."

Watching the landscape out my window: green, flat grasslands, stretching out into the horizon eternally.

We arrived at Standing Rock that night. I could see my breath in the cold air as we opened the car doors.

Katrina, a Brown woman with white streaks in her wiry black hair welcomed us into the midwives' tipi. Large colorful birds were painted on the outside of the tipi. Another midwife who had arrived that day, Mimi, blond and short, greeted us. She planned to live at Standing Rock for a month. Inside the tipi was warm, with the smell of burning wood emanating from the black, metal stove standing on bricks in the center of the tipi. The stove's smoke rose through the makeshift metal chimney into the night.

Carolina remarked that there were five midwives at the camp, the most there had ever been.

I followed Bev to visit our neighbors. The midwives' space sat next to a green army tent, which was the medics' center, and next to the large wellness center tent that was filled with herbs in glass containers on shelves and tables.

After a couple of failed attempts, Bev and I managed to set up my tent. I dragged the sleeping bags from the car and tried to make Aza's and my small shelter cozy.

Aza put her hands on her hips, "Can I walk around and explore?"

"Sure," I said, "just don't go too far." I handed her the flashlight.

"I know, we are the blue tent next to the big tipi." So matter-of-fact.

"Exactly." She was always good at navigation.

She returned fifteen minutes later saying how beautiful it all was and how it reminded her of the revolution in Cairo. I nodded, "The way it was at night with all the tents and flags and fires and city lights . . ."

She fell asleep in her sleeping bag while I read the anthology *Sisters of the Revolution*. I grabbed my flashlight and walked around the camp, feeling nostalgic for Tahrir Square nights at the height of the Arab Spring. Now, I was on the Great Plains. Sparse trees and the sky overflowing with stars.

I returned to our tent and struggled to sleep in the bitter cold. Around 5:00 a.m., I had gotten about thirty minutes of sleep. An insistent call to prayer over a loudspeaker kept jolting me awake. "Time to get up and pray. This is what we are here for. Pray for the water. Pray for strength to fight against the black snake. Pray for the land. Pray to wakan tanka. To pray. To pray. To pray."

When I heard mumbling conversations, I grabbed my mug, poured myself fresh coffee in the midwives' tipi.

I rolled a cigarette. Katrina, her cheeks ruddy and brown, joined me for a smoke in the fresh air. She pointed to tents being set up a few yards away, "Here come the weekend warriors. That's what people here call the folks who just come to camp for the weekend, like you guys . . . Some people use the term as an insult, but we need weekend warriors too."

I watched the clouds moved across the sky, the sunlight warmed the austere prairie. Grasslands with a few trees dotted the landscape. Small hills on the distant horizon. When the clouds returned, the wind blew electric. Even though it had been so cold the night before, the day warmed up until it was in the mid-'60s.

Our campsite was a part of Oceti Sakowin, main camp, where many of the major institutions of the Standing Rock resistance had been set up. Near the entrance to Oceti Sakowin was main circle, which held the sacred fire and the announcement board. Meetings at main circle were held twice a day at 10:00 a.m. and 4:00 p.m. Oceti was also where the medic tents, midwives' tent, wellness tent, two-spirit camp and the donation tents, aka the "mall," were.

One of the day's projects was to build two yurts closer to main circle and Red Warrior camp. One yurt for the midwives and the other for the medics. As the adults began pulling wood and tarps from the truck, I arranged for their kids hanging around the campsite to play soccer. There was Isa, thirteen years old. Aza was nine. Caya, a tall and pale woman with dark, curly hair, had brought her twins, who were seven and three-quarters. Another kid, from the building crew, was six years old and another was five. We stuck poles into the ground to make goal posts and Isa supervised the game with them.

As the kids were playing, a petite Brown person, Vara, and their child, Araksi, walked towards us. They had short punk bangs, stretched ears, large tattoos and said they were camping at Red Warrior camp. Araksi was small and quiet with long dreadlocks. We talked about single motherhood, about fathers who don't really parent, about radical people of color and indigeneity, about their experiences for the past three weeks at Red Warrior camp, their drive from O'odham territory to Standing Rock.

Bev walked up to Vara and me, announced there was an action happening at the front line and that I should take Isa. Aza said she didn't want to go, she wanted to finish her drawing in our little tent. I found Isa, and we caught a ride on the back of a pickup truck to the action. The sun was high as we approached a line of cops blocking our path to the con- struction sites. They were dressed in black military gear and holding batons. They didn't look at us, but out into nowhere. Around Isa and me, people chanted, prayed, offered tobacco to the earth, and yelled "Mni Wiconi." After about thirty minutes the leaders yelled, "We have prayed and now we are going to leave peacefully!" We turned around and walked away from the police, toward the trucks and cars on the dirt road and rode back to camp.

I met Carolina on my way to the campsite. "How was the action?" She asked.

"It was beautiful and short. A lot of prayers and chanting."

"Oh. That wasn't the real action." She told me that there had been a second action, parallel to the nonconfrontational action I had just attended. The parallel action had included warriors chaining themselves to the pipeline equipment and people were getting arrested. "Don't underestimate the warriors. Your action was a decoy for the real action. The warriors have strategies and maps." She smirked.

I nodded. "Well, I would expect them to have a strategy. And definitely hope they have maps . . ."

She turned to go to Red Warrior camp.

I went to our campsite and hung out with Aza for a bit and then walked to main circle to find extra blankets. Bev had dropped by our tent earlier with a couple of flannel blankets she had picked up at the "mall" and a down coat she had brought for me from Minneapolis. But I wanted to get more blankets, to make sure I slept that night. The mall, it turned out, was a series of tents on main circle where donations were housed. One tent was packed full of jackets and coats hanging and more piled in cardboard boxes. Another tent was full of scarves, hats, gloves, socks. Another piled four feet high with hundreds of blankets.

I returned to our campsite. Aza was playing with Caya's twins. Aza wanted to gather sticks and light them in the stove in the midwives' tipi. I handed her the long grill lighter and took a few minutes to arrange the blankets in our tent.

I heard two people talking outside of the tent, "Oh, Mai'a's kid is playing in the fire with two other children."

"Where is Mai'a?"

"I don't know."

"Well, I don't think the kids should be playing with the stove without adult supervision."

I finished lining the sleeping bags and rearranging our bags and reemerged outside.

"Mai'a, the kids are in there playing with fire."

"Yeah, I know."

"Well, let's not have the kids in the tipi alone. Without an adult."

I chuckled to myself. Yes, I let Aza "play with" fire. She had tended fires for years. She cooked basically by herself.

"Come on, Aza. Let's go explore. Plus, I want to find a decent cup of coffee."

The wind blew fierce over the plains and pushed down our tent. When we returned to the campsite, Caya and I broke down the tent, leaving everything inside. I set the tent back up when the winds died a couple of hours later. All day, airplanes and helicopters circled. A constant, low-level buzz permeated the air. There had been almost no cell phone reception at the camps for months, because soon after the water protectors had arrived, the signal was constantly scrambled. The only place for reliable service was on "Facebook hill" on the other side of camp.

Aza fell asleep early that night. I crawled into the sleeping bag with a pink rubber hot-water bottle. Outside, the soft rustle of conversations in the distance. I put on two pairs of socks and then placed a hand-warmer in between the layers of socks. I zipped up the down coat. Put on a pair of ear-warmers. And kept my hat on. Cozy. Opened my book of short stories, swallowed a tablet of melatonin, and fell asleep.

Saturday morning, I awoke to the English mixed with Lakota and other Indigenous languages washing over me. "Wake up. Your warriors need you. It is time. This is what you came for. To go defend our water. Time to protect our water. We must be strong."

I remembered when Vara, the petite Brown mama, and I had talked with an elder Lakota man Friday. He said that part of his work was to call everyone to ceremony. "It is important to pray. To start the day with prayer. With a reminder of why we are here . . . We go down to the river, a line of folks walking down to the river and the women lead the blessing of the water. That is our work."

Vara said softly, "I talked about this in Red Warrior camp, that we needed to pray more." Araksi played on the ground with a stick next to them.

The elder went on, "Now is the time to prepare for winter snow. We are from here and we are used to winter and the snow and now we have to teach the rest of folks how to deal with it. This is another role for the elders." I realized from him and Vara how much the frontline warriors needed to know how to create strong disciplined teams, how morning prayer supported one's focus and inner strength. Ceremony, fire, song, chant, rededication to the earth, good food were all necessary to win. He reminded us that a lot of the elders were military veterans and knew how to strategize against state violence. I nodded and thought, yes, and a lot of the mamas were community organizers.

That morning I woke to the loudspeaker prayers and got dressed to go to ceremony, while Aza slept. But as I stood outside of my tent watching folks walk toward the road, a whispered voice kept telling me: Go back to bed. Don't pray. Sleep.

I fell asleep for a few more hours. I woke up to a couple of midwives talking outside the tipi, put on my boots, greeted them and poured myself a cup of coffee.

I sat with the other midwives outside on camping chairs smoking their cigarettes and enjoying the morning coffee. They said that fifty-three people had been arrested at the morning prayer.

Katrina walked up, "That was a shitshow. A pure shitshow." The water protectors had walked up to the construction site, praying and singing, and the police had met them with riot gear, pepper spray, and batons and began grabbing and arresting people en masse as the water protectors tried to run away. At least eighty people had been arrested she said.

"Damn," I said, "and I'm so glad I didn't go."

Over a cigarette, I mentioned to Mimi that having organized childcare would be helpful at the camp.

Mimi replied, "Oh I just thought everybody here was into free range."

"Hmmm . . . really? 'Cause I think there is a school here. So there must be some interest in the kids' experiences. Do you know where it is?"

She shook her head. Mimi had been a midwife in east Africa and wanted to work for Doctors Without Borders. She had spent the morning working in the medic tent treating the wounded warriors.

Mimi and Mel had announced earlier that morning that the kids were no longer allowed to play in the tipi. They had found some small, easily replaced part of one of the lamps broken and decided to blame it on the younger kids. I shrugged.

Mimi and Mel were mothers, too, but they had left their kids back home. Aza and I got breakfast from a nearby large kitchen. They had run out of cereal, so we ate tortillas with eggs, beans, tomatoes, and short rice. Aza drank water and I sipped coffee with powdered milk and listened to the buzz of people around us.

Caya, the twins, and I went looking for the school. Aza decided to stay by the campsite and whittle branches outside the tent. "Okay, babe." I said. "Be safe."

A large, green army tent and a couple more nearby tipis housed the school. As we walked up, giggling kids ran in and out of the main tent. Two kids stood, coloring at a wooden table. It was Saturday. I had expected the school to be closed but the energy was vibrant.

The main tent was dark inside, and large. A wall of bookshelves, the genres and reading levels labeled. Lacrosse sticks piled in one cardboard box. Soccer balls in another.

The teacher, Miguel, introduced himself. It turned out he was from Ecuador.

"Really? I worked for teleSUR English in Quito last year. Where in Ecuador are you from?"

"Cuenca."

"I hear it's beautiful."

In 2014 and 2015, I explained, Aza and I had lived in Quito as I worked for teleSUR English, a Venezuelan global news agency. We had fallen in love with Ecuador, the landscape and the sweet cultures. We talked a bit about Ecuadorian politics, Latin American socialism, and the utter beauty of Ecuador. Caya had never been to South America, but her mother was Venezuelan.

Miguel then explained how the school worked. It was open from Monday through Friday, 10:00 a.m. to 4:00 p.m. They began the day with prayers and then taught Lakota values. After that there were level-appropriate courses in reading, writing, mathematics, physical education, and art. They had about thirty to forty students attending now and they expected to have about fifteen students during the winter.

The air on the plains was dry. It didn't rain. The brown grass laid flat on the ground. Snow was coming soon.

I returned to the campsite and checked in with Aza. Mimi offered us a ride to Red Warrior camp. She needed to return a drill bit to one of the guys there. Aza and I got in her four-wheel-drive Jeep that she had driven from Oregon to Standing Rock, leaving behind her husband and kids.

When she parked she said, "Aza should stay in the truck."

"Why?"

"Because children aren't allowed in the Red Warrior camp."

"Are you sure? Because I met a mama yesterday who camps here and they have their child here . . ."

She shrugged. "I was told that children weren't supposed to be here."

"Huh. Okay. Aza, stay in the car for a few minutes. Let me see what's up."

"Okay, mama."

Mimi and I walked into the camp. There weren't as many women as there were in main camp. Folks looked like they were mainly in their twenties. More folks had an anarchist punk vibe: more piercings, deliberately ragged haircuts, dirty bandannas. They were working on one of several half-built wooden structures or gathering around one of the many fire pits.

We headed toward the less-populated back of the camp. Mimi stopped and said, "I think he's supposed to be back here, but it's a Native-only area."

"Oh, well, I'll go back and ask . . ."

"No. It's really only for Natives."

"Um . . . okay . . ."

She turned left and started walking toward one of the building projects. A black-haired warrior handed me a smooth, purple and gray shell. "For you, sister."

Mimi pointed to a large structure that had in front of it a whiteboard with what looked like the daily menu. "Red warrior camp has the best food."

I nodded, "I'll have to remember that."

I saw Araksi, playing with a couple of children a few feet from the kitchen on top of a makeshift wooden table and a couple of boxes.

They looked up at me and grinned, "Hey!"

"Hey, Araksi. Where's your mama?"

They pointed behind them.

Vara showed up after a few minutes.

"Hey! How are you?"

"Tired. I've been doing childcare. You know about all the arrests that happened this morning?"

"Yeah, we heard."

"They were saying that they wanted to do this big action and they wanted it to be Native-led. I thought it was not good for us to risk our Native warriors." I looked around and realized that the space was full of pale men.

"We lost so many of our warriors. At least hundred people." They pointed to another child. "Both of their parents were arrested."

"Damn. You know, there is another single mama who has twins and I bet that she'd be willing to help out. She runs a childcare back in Oregon. And we were talking about doing childcare and—wait, let me go get Aza, she's still in the car."

I walked to the jeep and asked Aza, "Babe, are you hungry? Come see if there's anything you want."

After we grabbed lunch and returned to our camp, we ran into Caya and her kids, and I told her about Vara and the child whose parents had been detained. Aza and I continued to walk around, making our way to the Red Warrior camp. As I was trying to work out how to help Vara with childcare, Caya and the twin girls arrived. Their wavy hair, posture, and energy reminded me of the horses they camped next to.

"Caya! I was just talking about you! What kismet!"

I turned to Vara, who reminded me of a bird. Slim strong wings.

We piled the kids onto a wagon. Caya, Vara, and the twins pulled them down the road to the midwifery campsite. A parade of kids. Laughing. Yelling. Making up games on the spot. They played in the field by the midwives' tipi while the sun set.

I had heard the midwives and medics talking about the Red Warriors' machismo. At sacred circle, the elder water protectors seemed ambivalent about the Red Warriors and their direct-action tactics. Several spoke for nonconfrontational prayer and ceremony being at the center of the struggle. A man who was a former member of the American Indian Movement asked that there should never be violence against the police officers or the pipeline. He said that it was violence that had caused the demise of AIM in the '70s. An elder woman said that passive resistance and faith in the ancestors' way was the only way to prevail.

The rhythm of life at Standing Rock reminded me of my time in the southern Hebron hills, off the electric grid and no running water. I spent my days talking with folks about their life stories and listening to their future visions. We drank hot tea, played with kids, ate meals, prayed, accompanied folks, and stared at the horizon as the sun set behind the rolling hills dotted with bison. We found a daily rhythm in the midst of police violence and the black snake.

That evening, Aza and I ate dinner at Red Warrior camp and listened to the bonfire conversations. Most of the warriors looked to be in their twenties and thirties.

After introductions, I asked one blond woman how long she had been at Standing Rock.

"Since August."

"And how long do you plan on staying?"

She looked at her colleagues and smirked, "Until . . ."

"Until we've won, you mean?"

She crossed her arms in front of her chest. "However long that takes . . ."

"Are you ready for winter?"

"We are getting there . . ."

Back and forth, the warriors talked about the action that morning, arrests, next steps, logistics. Over 140 people had been arrested. DAPL built a quarter of a mile of new pipeline daily and it was about seven miles away from main camp. At that rate, the black snake would reach Oceti Sakowin in less than a month. Time was running out and the warriors needed to find a way to stop the pipeline or the water protectors' battle would be lost.

I had heard contradictory reports about the morning's actions. It was good to hear the evaluations of the planning and execution from the warriors themselves. It reminded me of sitting in tents and cafés with the Tahrir Square activists as they had discussed protecting the shaky freedoms they had just won.

One person mentioned that there had been a child around the age of ten at the action and there had been a mama and a kid. "I just don't think that kids should be at something like that . . ."

"Yeah, I'm not arrestable, because I have Aza. And I wouldn't want to take her with me or get arrested and leave her here. We don't have that kind of backup in place in case I get arrested, so . . . yeah. But you know, if it did happen, it wouldn't be the first time Aza was in detention. I mean, it's not preferable. But seriously, Aza has been through so much, I would trust her to be up there on the front lines more than a lot of forty-year-olds. At least I know she's solid in the field."

They nodded, "Yeah, I can see that. I guess it is different if you grew up with it."

"Yeah," I went on, "I think that is the difference. We were in Cairo, Egypt, when the Arab Spring began. She's been tear-gassed more times . . . has dealt with police, has been in demos that turned violent. I mean, that is just stuff that happens if you lived in Cairo back then. So . . . yeah, I don't worry about her too much. I'm protective, and it is way preferable that we don't deal with it at all, which is why I wasn't arrestable this morning. But we can give more credit to kids and to mamas, you know. It was the youth who started this resistance in the first place."

Caya and her daughters asked Aza if she wanted to come hang out with her daughters in their tent and watch a DVD. That way I could stay by the fire and talk some more.

Aza had said she felt confident returning to our tent by herself. But now she was excited to go watch a DVD. I thanked Caya, sipped my coffee, shivered at the blast of smoke from the bonfire, and talked with warriors about moving the camp to the front lines in the upcoming days.

That evening Mimi, Bev, and I sat outside the midwives' tipi, smoking cigarettes and talking about midwifery, medic work, Indigenous organizing, working in east Africa and being mamas.

Sunday morning, the call to prayers woke me up again. I followed the sound in the predawn cold.

A loose circle of people gathered around the sacred fire.

"We are the prophecies of our ancestors. They told us that there would come a time when we had to gather and fight. It is our time to protect our water, protect our land, our sovereignty, our sacred places, our children, our future." I stood staring into the fire, rocking slightly to keep warm. People came to the fire and tossed handfuls of tobacco and cypress into the fire. The sky was dark, but the stars were fading. Our fists were raised. The prayers, ceremonies, and earth were with us. A cosmological power, intimate and vast, was holding us, guiding us in this five-hundred-year war of colonization, genocide, and theft.

When I was around four years old, one warm evening after the sun had set and the sky was misty blue, I stood on the blacktop driveway with my father as he smoked a cigarette. These were the days before the paranoia and schizophrenia had taken over his nervous system, the days when he still talked to me about what he loved: science and books and music, when he didn't live in a world of fear and invisible predators. He pointed to the first bright stars blinking into view and said, "The sun is a star just like all the other stars, but it's much closer than all these other and stars. That is why it is so bright" In a flash, I saw how in the mornings, all the individual stars gathered together in one large circle to create the sun and make the day bright and at dusk the stars blew apart like dandelion seeds and scattered across the dark nighttime sky. And then in the morning they came together again like the breath. Inhale. Sun. Exhale. Stars.

I watched the sacred embers scatter out to the sky, surrounded by the hum of prayers and white clouds of breaths, and remembered the Arab Spring revolutionaries who had become one more diaspora. Spread over the globe. Away and toward each other. Communities that had been nourished by mothering were torn apart by violence. What is a revolution if they cannot even stand in public in the same place? Now we know each other through social media, digital moments of meaning. A new article, a new tweet, a new cartoon, a new poem—reminds us what tribe we belong to. And remembering feels violent, destroying us from the inside out. For a moment, we remember what it felt like to stand in the same square, the same city, the same continent and fight.

The Egyptian revolution had mutated from "the people demand the fall of the regime" to, as the rapper Jean Grae had predicted about revolutions, "everybody just out for self." Exile.

And after the exile? We wandered the earth.

I first went to Palestine, hoping to support the space in which Palestinians could resist annihilation and weave paradise.

But no place or people were paradise.

Paradise was those moments when in my bones I felt that I was connected to everything in the multiverse across time and space. More than an endorphin rush, it was a full-throated "yes" to the present moment. It was when I gave myself permission to love, to feel warm toward the world, to accept it all, just as it was, like during the Palestinian Intifada, the Egyptian revolution and while staring into holy fires of Standing Rock.

But other times I just felt strange and alone: in Israeli detention with Aza, in the violence of the Egyptian counter-revolution, when I struggled to find a place for Aza and me among the Standing Rock encampment.

Whether I was mothering children or revolutions, I learned that the only way to do it well was for me to show up as my full, genuine self with all my glorious flaws and strengths and offer what I had, whether it be my body standing in the way of violence, my writing and photographs, my strange stories, an extra set of hands, a love for hip hop and books, for liberation and mothering. I fought for whom and what I loved, made mistakes, mourned, rested, healed, and then I got up and did it again. This was paradise.

Mothering had shown me how to show up every day for another human being. Aza had seen me at my worst and my best everything in between. So had our comrades over the years. We were artists and lovers and children, teachers, activists and mamas flung across the globe. We had held each other and betrayed each other, ran away from and toward each other. And for a few moments, here and there, in peace and war, we had made paradise with each other, by simply being present to the extraordinary fact that we were alive.

And there was paradise, I finally realized that morning as I watched the smoke climb to overcast black sky, in the diasporic experience. Even in exile.

Inhale. Sun. Exhale. Stars.

The elder in front of the sacred fire intoned, "We know what we are fighting for and that is why we will win."

During the prayers elders sometimes described "warriors" and "mothers" as two separate roles. The role of the warriors, they said, was to protect the mothers and children, the water, the earth, the vulnerable and the role of mothers was to support the warriors.

The sun cut over the horizon. The warriors who were going to the front line that morning got in their cars and trucks and rode to fight for the survival of the earth and its peoples. Caya had shown up at the ceremony with her twins and had asked me to look after them as she went to join the action for a few minutes. "No problem." The mamas I knew were strong because they nourished and nurtured, but also protected and fought in defense of life.

The twins and I sat next to the elder tending the fire. We sang impromptu blues songs and drank cold coffee.

As I was walking from the sacred fire back to our tent, a child who was playing on some painted tree stumps yelled to me, "What does your hair look like?"

The child was petite with dark brown skin and was wearing a knit cap.

I paused and asked, "What does your hair look like?"

They pulled off their cap and long, dark, messy, wavy hair tumbled down their shoulders.

I smiled, pulled off my cap and shook my hair loose.

"You have dreadlocks!"

"Yep."

Another child on the stumps asked, "What is the color in your hair?"

"Yarn."

I stuffed my hair back into my cap, waved goodbye, wondering if they were also Black and Indigenous.

This was my first time being at a pan-Native gathering. And like going to a Black gathering, especially in the Americas, the full spectrum of shades and color, browns, reds, pinks, blacks, yellows, pales, and darks were all present.

The late morning turned windy and blustery. The large sky blanketed in clouds. The medics and warriors informed us that we needed to move the midwifery center away from the relative safety of main camp and up to the front lines of the battle. The warriors had a new strategy. At noon, when Bev and I left, Mimi was the only midwife in the camp. The other two midwives, Katrina and Mel, had left the day before. Mimi assured us, wrapped up in her winter coat and thick gloves, that she was going to be fine.

As Bev drove us away from the Standing Rock reservation, we saw police cars with Minneapolis insignia driving toward Standing Rock. I kept checking the news on my phone and read that North Dakota had invoked the Emergency Management Assistance Compact, a statute that allowed North Dakota to coordinate emergency personnel in an emergency. Since the governor of North Dakota had that summer declared a state of emergency at Standing Rock, he had invoked EMAC to ask for police officers from neighboring states to assist the North Dakota police in stopping the water protectors from defending their land.

When I returned home after the long car ride with Bev, Isa, and Aza, I looked online to see if there was any information about traditional Lakota culture and gender roles. I found a blog post written by Russell Means, an elder leader of AIM, in which he wrote in 2006:

> My People, Lakota, also known as Sioux Indians, are Matriarchal. I was raised in a Matriarchal home, and when I married, I married into Matriarchal homes. I know my history and I know my People, therefore I can speak about the values and complexity of Matriarchy.
>
> Matriarchy is a balanced society. Now listen very carefully, and please attempt to grasp the big picture. In our Matriarchal society, all the sexes celebrate our strengths. We are a society completely devoted to not harming another living being's feelings; be it an insect, a tree, our Grandmother, the Earth, or anyone that lives.

Aza and I had spent so much time in resistance communities. After nine years, I was used to explaining why my young daughter was with me, despite the risk, and that I carefully considered risk and safety for both of us, and how deeply I believed in the resistance. "I mean, Aza was conceived in the West Bank during the Israeli-Hezbollah war, while I was working as a journalist and I would have given birth to her there if the Israeli border security hadn't have kicked me out . . ."

In 2010, I wrote in a bio about myself, "She has dedicated her body and life to stopping by any means necessary and possible the violence (whether it be state, military, communitarian, medical, domestic, etc.) that threatens our survival on this earth and to co-creating with you revolutionary, liberatory communities."

Sitting with the warriors reminded me of those long nights sitting in crowded living rooms with Tahrir kids in the heady days in early 2011, of sitting on desert Palestinian hillsides in the autumn of 2004.

As a Black woman, I had been safer walking the dirt roads of at-Tuwani than in the cities of Hebron and Jerusalem. In the early days of revolutionary Tahrir, I had felt safer than

I had ever felt before in downtown Cairo. It was only on the evening when Mubarak was ousted from office and celebrations erupted en masse downtown that we heard the first reports of women being sexually assaulted in Tahrir Square. And I felt a similar safety at Standing Rock, even safer than I felt in the small lily-white conservative Minnesota town where we lived. In revolutionary encampments, I didn't feel the need to apologize for my existence, for my Black skin and wild hair, for my confident walk and radical politics.

Standing Rock didn't seem to be as matriarchal as Russell Means described, but I found more openness toward my daughter and I among the warriors, especially the Native warriors, than I did with white-dominated parts of main camp. I felt welcomed and at ease at the Red Warrior camp and didn't encounter the level of machismo others talked about. Red Warrior camp had more nonwhite people than the midwifery and medic centers. From the night I had bought a pregnancy test, it had been primarily white folks, even white mothers, who had declared that I couldn't be a revolutionary and a mama. Actual revolutionary communities had usually welcomed me, in part, because I was a mother.

Over the next few days, I was glued to social media as shaky reports, live streaming videos, tweets, and pictures trickled in, as the warriors fought against the police. They had moved the main organs of the main camp very close to the construction site, the front lines, where Isa and I had demonstrated a few days before. They blocked the construction site, trying to stop the pipeline. The police attacked the water protectors and destroyed the front line camp's tipis and tents.

There were a lot of arguments among the water protectors about whether the warriors' decision to move to the front lines would unnecessarily escalate the violence. Some folks said that the warriors were violating their nonviolent principles, but the police's outsized violent response led to the struggle against DAPL becoming international news.

I sprinkled tobacco and water on the ground. I lit a cigarette and prayed for the mama warriors holding down the front lines.

May they know paradise.

Acknowledgments

It has been such a gift and pleasure to write this book. There are so many people over the years and decades who helped to make this book a reality.

First and foremost thank you to my daughter, Aza Theresa, who teaches me so much. She came along with her mama on our wild adventures and has been such a happy-go-lucky, flexible, perceptive child.

To my parents, Deborah and Nat, my younger brother, Safi. And especially to my grandmother, Essie Mae Lowery, who always encouraged me to write and read as much as possible and who said in the face of so many family members' doubt that she thought it was a "good thing" that I go to Palestine.

To Cal, Walt, and Heather.

To Ariel Gore, who has been such a gracious mentor and hip mama inspiration.

To Mary Scott Boria and Dorothy Friesen. To Aurora, Joelle, Annie, Emily, Bruno and Vanessa, Melanie, Ben, Sam and Tilde, James and Steve and Rania, Mary Jo and Sharon, Jeanette.

To Alexis and China, Leah Lakshmi Piepzna-Samarasinha, Vikki Law, Lasara, Jenny F, and Alexis De Veaux.

To the revolutionary mamas, the tender lovers, the freedom fighters, the dawn dancers, the babysitters, the sisters-in-arms, the martyrs, the street artists, the local journalists, the mentors, the matriarchs, the Indigenous poets, the bartenders, the strange friends, the newborn babies, the haters, the innocents, the idealists, the anarchists, the queer kids, the lost ones, the ancestors, the dreamers, the atheists who bow their head in prayer, the elders who refuse to ever bow again. Look, y'all, we here in paradise. We made it.

About the authors

Mai'a Williams is a writer, visual artist, and birth worker and has worked and lived in Mexico, Palestine, east Africa, Egypt, Germany, Ecuador, and the United States. In 2008, she published the *Revolutionary Motherhood* anthology zine and the corresponding group blog, a collection of writing and visual art about mothering on the margins, which became the inspiration for the book *Revolutionary Mothering: Love on the Front Lines*, which she coedited. Williams is also the author of two books of poetry, *No God but Ghosts* and *Monsters and Other Silent Creatures*.

Ariel Gore is the founding editor of *Hip Mama* and the author of many books of fiction and nonfiction, including the critically acclaimed novel *We Were Witches*. She has won an American Alternative Press Award, the LAMBDA, the Rainbow Book Award, and an Arizona–New Mexico Book Award. Her writing has appeared in hundreds of publications including the *Rumpus*, *Psychology Today*, and the *San Francisco Chronicle*.

ABOUT PM PRESS

PM Press was founded at the end of 2007 by a small collection of folks with decades of publishing, media, and organizing experience. PM Press co-conspirators have published and distributed hundreds of books, pamphlets, CDs, and DVDs. Members of PM have founded enduring book fairs, spearheaded victorious tenant organizing campaigns, and worked closely with bookstores, academic conferences, and even rock bands to deliver political and challenging ideas to all walks of life. We're old enough to know what we're doing and young enough to know what's at stake.

We seek to create radical and stimulating fiction and nonfiction books, pamphlets, T-shirts, visual and audio materials to entertain, educate, and inspire you. We aim to distribute these through every available channel with every available technology—whether that means you are seeing anarchist classics at our bookfair stalls, reading our latest vegan cookbook at the café, downloading geeky fiction e-books, or digging new music and timely videos from our website.

PM Press is always on the lookout for talented and skilled volunteers, artists, activists, and writers to work with. If you have a great idea for a project or can contribute in some way, please get in touch.

PM Press
PO Box 23912
Oakland, CA 94623
www.pmpress.org

PM Press in Europe
europe@pmpress.org
www.pmpress.org.uk

FRIENDS OF PM PRESS

These are indisputably momentous times—the financial system is melting down globally and the Empire is stumbling. Now more than ever there is a vital need for radical ideas.

In the years since its founding—and on a mere shoestring—PM Press has risen to the formidable challenge of publishing and distributing knowledge and entertainment for the struggles ahead. With over 300 releases to date, we have published an impressive and stimulating array of literature, art, music, politics, and culture. Using every available medium, we've succeeded in connecting those hungry for ideas and information to those putting them into practice.

Friends of PM allows you to directly help impact, amplify, and revitalize the discourse and actions of radical writers, filmmakers, and artists. It provides us with a stable foundation from which we can build upon our early successes and provides a much-needed subsidy for the materials that can't necessarily pay their own way. You can help make that happen—and receive every new title automatically delivered to your door once a month—by joining as a Friend of PM Press. And, we'll throw in a free T-shirt when you sign up.

Here are your options:

- **$30 a month** Get all books and pamphlets plus 50% discount on all webstore purchases

- **$40 a month** Get all PM Press releases (including CDs and DVDs) plus 50% discount on all webstore purchases

- **$100 a month** Superstar—Everything plus PM merchandise, free downloads, and 50% discount on all webstore purchases

For those who can't afford $30 or more a month, we have **Sustainer Rates** at $15, $10 and $5. Sustainers get a free PM Press T-shirt and a 50% discount on all purchases from our website.

Your Visa or Mastercard will be billed once a month, until you tell us to stop. Or until our efforts succeed in bringing the revolution around. Or the financial meltdown of Capital makes plastic redundant. Whichever comes first.

Revolutionary Mothering: Love on the Front Lines

Edited by Alexis Pauline Gumbs,
China Martens, and Mai'a Williams
with a preface by Loretta J. Ross

ISBN: 978-1-62963-110-3
$17.95   272 pages

Inspired by the legacy of radical and queer
black feminists of the 1970s and '80s,
Revolutionary Mothering places marginalized mothers of color at the
center of a world of necessary transformation. The challenges we face as
movements working for racial, economic, reproductive, gender, and food
justice, as well as anti-violence, anti-imperialist, and queer liberation
are the same challenges that many mothers face every day. Oppressed
mothers create a generous space for life in the face of life-threatening
limits, activate a powerful vision of the future while navigating tangible
concerns in the present, move beyond individual narratives of choice
toward collective solutions, live for more than ourselves, and remain
accountable to a future that we cannot always see. *Revolutionary
Mothering* is a movement-shifting anthology committed to birthing new
worlds, full of faith and hope for what we can raise up together.

Contributors include June Jordan, Malkia A. Cyril, Esteli Juarez, Cynthia
Dewi Oka, Fabiola Sandoval, Sumayyah Talibah, Victoria Law, Tara
Villalba, Lola Mondragón, Christy NaMee Eriksen, Norma Angelica
Marrun, Vivian Chin, Rachel Broadwater, Autumn Brown, Layne Russell,
Noemi Martinez, Katie Kaput, alba onofrio, Gabriela Sandoval, Cheryl
Boyce Taylor, Ariel Gore, Claire Barrera, Lisa Factora-Borchers, Fabielle
Georges, H. Bindy K. Kang, Terri Nilliasca, Irene Lara, Panquetzani,
Mamas of Color Rising, tk karakashian tunchez, Arielle Julia Brown,
Lindsey Campbell, Micaela Cadena, and Karen Su.

*"This collection is a treat for anyone that sees class and that needs to learn
more about the experiences of women of color (and who doesn't?!). There
is no dogma here, just fresh ideas and women of color taking on capitalism,
anti-racist, anti-sexist theory-building that is rooted in the most primal
of human connections, the making of two people from the body of one:
mothering."*
—Barbara Jensen, author of *Reading Classes: On Culture and Classism in
America*

Birth Work as Care Work: Stories from Activist Birth Communities

Alana Apfel, with a foreword by Loretta J. Ross, preface by Victoria Law, and introduction by Silvia Federici

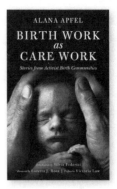

ISBN: 978-1-62963-151-6
$14.95   128 pages

Birth Work as Care Work presents a vibrant collection of stories and insights from the front lines of birth activist communities. The personal has once more become political, and birth workers, supporters, and doulas now find themselves at the fore of collective struggles for freedom and dignity.

The author, herself a scholar and birth justice organiser, provides a unique platform to explore the political dynamics of birth work; drawing connections between birth, reproductive labor, and the struggles of caregiving communities today. Articulating a politics of care work in and through the reproductive process, the book brings diverse voices into conversation to explore multiple possibilities and avenues for change.

At a moment when agency over our childbirth experiences is increasingly centralized in the hands of professional elites, *Birth Work as Care Work* presents creative new ways to reimagine the trajectory of our reproductive processes. Most importantly, the contributors present new ways of thinking about the entire life cycle, providing a unique and creative entry point into the essence of all human struggle—the struggle over the reproduction of life itself.

"I love this book, all of it. The polished essays and the interviews with birth workers dare to take on the deepest questions of human existence."
—Carol Downer, cofounder of the Feminist Women's Heath Centers of California and author of *A Woman's Book of Choices*

"This volume provides theoretically rich, practical tools for birth and other care workers to collectively and effectively fight capitalism and the many intersecting processes of oppression that accompany it. Birth Work as Care Work forcefully and joyfully reminds us that the personal is political, a lesson we need now more than ever."
—Adrienne Pine, author of *Working Hard, Drinking Hard: On Violence and Survival in Honduras*

Witches, Witch-Hunting, and Women

Silvia Federici

ISBN: 978-1-62963-568-2
$14.00   120 pages

We are witnessing a new surge of interpersonal and institutional violence against women, including new witch hunts. This surge of violence has occurred alongside an expansion of capitalist social relations. In this new work that revisits some of the main themes of *Caliban and the Witch*, Silvia Federici examines the root causes of these developments and outlines the consequences for the women affected and their communities. She argues that, no less than the witch hunts in sixteenth- and seventeenth-century Europe and the "New World," this new war on women is a structural element of the new forms of capitalist accumulation. These processes are founded on the destruction of people's most basic means of reproduction. Like at the dawn of capitalism, what we discover behind today's violence against women are processes of enclosure, land dispossession, and the remolding of women's reproductive activities and subjectivity.

As well as an investigation into the causes of this new violence, the book is also a feminist call to arms. Federici's work provides new ways of understanding the methods in which women are resisting victimization and offers a powerful reminder that reconstructing the memory of the past is crucial for the struggles of the present.

"It is good to think with Silvia Federici, whose clarity of analysis and passionate vision come through in essays that chronicle enclosure and dispossession, witch-hunting and other assaults against women, in the present, no less than the past. It is even better to act armed with her insights."
—Eileen Boris, Hull Professor of Feminist Studies, University of California, Santa Barbara

"Silvia Federici's new book offers a brilliant analysis and forceful denunciation of the violence directed towards women and their communities. Her focus moves between women criminalized as witches both at the dawn of capitalism and in contemporary globalization. Federici has updated the material from her well-known book Caliban and the Witch *and brings a spotlight to the current resistance and alternatives being pursued by women and their communities through struggle."*
—Massimo De Angelis, professor of political economy, University of East London

Re-enchanting the World: Feminism and the Politics of the Commons

Silvia Federici with a Foreword by Peter Linebaugh

ISBN: 978-1-62963-569-9
$19.95   240 pages

Silvia Federici is one of the most important contemporary theorists of capitalism and feminist movements. In this collection of her work spanning over twenty years, she provides a detailed history and critique of the politics of the commons from a feminist perspective. In her clear and combative voice, Federici provides readers with an analysis of some of the key issues and debates in contemporary thinking on this subject.

Drawing on rich historical research, she maps the connections between the previous forms of enclosure that occurred with the birth of capitalism and the destruction of the commons and the "new enclosures" at the heart of the present phase of global capitalist accumulation. Considering the commons from a feminist perspective, this collection centers on women and reproductive work as crucial to both our economic survival and the construction of a world free from the hierarchies and divisions capital has planted in the body of the world proletariat. Federici is clear that the commons should not be understood as happy islands in a sea of exploitative relations but rather autonomous spaces from which to challenge the existing capitalist organization of life and labor.

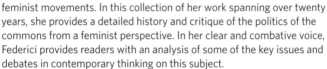

"Silvia Federici's theoretical capacity to articulate the plurality that fuels the contemporary movement of women in struggle provides a true toolbox for building bridges between different features and different people."
—Massimo De Angelis, professor of political economy, University of East London

"Silvia Federici's work embodies an energy that urges us to rejuvenate struggles against all types of exploitation and, precisely for that reason, her work produces a common: a common sense of the dissidence that creates a community in struggle."
—Maria Mies, coauthor of *Ecofeminism*

Revolution at Point Zero: Housework, Reproduction, and Feminist Struggle

Silvia Federici

ISBN: 978-1-60486-333-8
$15.95   208 pages

Written between 1974 and 2012, *Revolution at Point Zero* collects forty years of research and theorizing on the nature of housework, social reproduction, and women's struggles on this terrain—to escape it, to better its conditions, to reconstruct it in ways that provide an alternative to capitalist relations.

Indeed, as Federici reveals, behind the capitalist organization of work and the contradictions inherent in "alienated labor" is an explosive ground zero for revolutionary practice upon which are decided the daily realities of our collective reproduction.

Beginning with Federici's organizational work in the Wages for Housework movement, the essays collected here unravel the power and politics of wide but related issues including the international restructuring of reproductive work and its effects on the sexual division of labor, the globalization of care work and sex work, the crisis of elder care, the development of affective labor, and the politics of the commons.

"Finally we have a volume that collects the many essays that over a period of four decades Silvia Federici has written on the question of social reproduction and women's struggles on this terrain. While providing a powerful history of the changes in the organization of reproductive labor, Revolution at Point Zero *documents the development of Federici's thought on some of the most important questions of our time: globalization, gender relations, the construction of new commons."*
—Mariarosa Dalla Costa, author of *Women and the Subversion of the Community*

Rad Families: A Celebration

Edited by Tomas Moniz
with a Foreword by Ariel Gore

ISBN: 978-1-62963-230-8
$19.95   296 pages

Rad Families: A Celebration honors the messy,
the painful, the playful, the beautiful, the
myriad ways we create families. This is not
an anthology of experts, or how-to articles on
perfect parenting; it often doesn't even try to
provide answers. Instead, the writers strive to
be honest and vulnerable in sharing their stories and experiences, their
failures and their regrets.

Gathering parents and writers from diverse communities, it explores
the process of getting pregnant from trans birth to adoption, grapples
with issues of racism and police brutality, probes raising feminists and
feminist parenting. It plumbs the depths of empty nesting and letting go.

Some contributors are recognizable authors and activists but most are
everyday parents working and loving and trying to build a better world
one diaper change at a time. It's a book that reminds us all that we are
not alone, that community can help us get through the difficulties, can,
in fact, make us better people. It's a celebration, join us!

Contributors include Jonas Cannon, Ian MacKaye, Burke Stansbury,
Danny Goot, Simon Knaphus, Artnoose, Welch Canavan, Daniel Muro
LaMere, Jennifer Lewis, Zach Ellis, Alicia Dornadic, Jesse Palmer, Mindi
J., Carla Bergman, Tasnim Nathoo, Rachel Galindo, Robert Liu-Trujillo,
Dawn Caprice, Shawn Taylor, D.A. Begay, Philana Dollin, Airial Clark,
Allison Wolfe, Roger Porter, cubbie rowland-storm, Annakai & Rob
Geshlider, Jeremy Adam Smith, Frances Hardinge, Jonathan Shipley,
Bronwyn Davies Glover, Amy Abugo Ongiri, Mike Araujo, Craig Elliott,
Eleanor Wohlfeiler, Scott Hoshida, Plinio Hernandez, Madison Young,
Nathan Torp, Sasha Vodnik, Jessie Susannah, Krista Lee Hanson, Carvell
Wallace, Dani Burlison, Brian Whitman, scott winn, Kermit Playfoot,
Chris Crass, and Zora Moniz.

*"Rad dads, rad families, rad children. These stories show us that we are not
alone. That we don't have all the answers. That we are all learning."*
—Nikki McClure, illustrator, author, parent

Don't Leave Your Friends Behind: Concrete Ways to Support Families in Social Justice Movements and Communities

Edited by Victoria Law and China Martens

ISBN: 978–1–60486–396–3
$17.95   256 pages

Don't Leave Your Friends Behind is a collection of concrete tips, suggestions, and narratives on ways that non-parents can support parents, children, and caregivers in their communities, social movements, and collective processes. *Don't Leave Your Friends Behind* focuses on issues affecting children and caregivers within the larger framework of social justice, mutual aid, and collective liberation.

How do we create new, nonhierarchical structures of support and mutual aid, and include all ages in the struggle for social justice? There are many books on parenting, but few on being a good community member and a good ally to parents, caregivers, and children as we collectively build a strong all-ages culture of resistance. Any group of parents will tell you how hard their struggles are and how they are left out, but no book focuses on how allies can address issues of caretakers' and children's oppression. Many well-intentioned childless activists don't interact with young people on a regular basis and don't know how. *Don't Leave Your Friends Behind* provides them with the resources and support to get started.

Contributors include: The Bay Area Childcare Collective, Ramsey Beyer, Rozalinda Borcilă, Mariah Boone, Marianne Bullock, Lindsey Campbell, Briana Cavanaugh, CRAP! Collective, a de la maza pérez tamayo, Ingrid DeLeon, Clayton Dewey, David Gilbert, A.S. Givens, Jason Gonzales, Tiny (aka Lisa Gray-Garcia), Jessica Hoffman, Heather Jackson, Rahula Janowski, Sine Hwang Jensen, Agnes Johnson, Simon Knaphus, Victoria Law, London Pro-Feminist Men's Group, Amariah Love, Oluko Lumumba, mama raccoon, Mamas of Color Rising/Young Women United, China Martens, Noemi Martinez, Kathleen McIntyre, Stacey Milbern, Jessica Mills, Tomas Moniz, Coleen Murphy, Maegan 'la Mamita Mala' Ortiz, Traci Picard, Amanda Rich, Fabiola Sandoval, Cynthia Ann Schemmer, Mikaela Shafer, Mustafa Shakur, Kate Shapiro, Jennifer Silverman, Harriet Moon Smith, Mariahadessa Ekere Tallie, Darran White Tilghman, Jessica Trimbath, Max Ventura, and Mari Villaluna.

The Future Generation: The Zine-Book for Subculture Parents, Kids, Friends & Others

China Martens

ISBN: 978-1-62963-450-0
$22.00   240 pages

China Martens started her pioneering mamazine *The Future Generation* in 1990. She was a young anarchist punk rock mother who didn't feel that the mamas in her community had enough support, so she began publishing articles on radical parenting in an age before the internet.

The anthology of her zine, *The Future Generation: The Zine-Book for Subculture Parents, Kids, Friends & Others*, was first printed in 2007 and has been out of print for many years. Covering sixteen years, it uses individual issues as chapters, focusing on personal writing, and retaining the character of a zine that changed over the years—from her daughter's birth to teenagehood and beyond.

We are proud to present a tenth-anniversary edition including a new afterword by China's grown daughter, Clover. *The Future Generation* remains a timeless resource for parents, caregivers, and those who care about them. Though first published in the 1990s, many of the essays and observations—about parenting, children, and surviving in a hostile political climate—still ring true today. The next four years are going to be especially demanding for those trying to balance parenting, politics, and survival. We're going to need the voices and experiences in *The Future Generation* now more than ever.

"The original punk parent zine."
—Ariel Gore, *Hip Mama*

"Martens has been writing since long before the mommy wars were a media trope, but her work is a powerful response to punditry casting institutional and political problems as personal issues of 'work-life balance' for mothers (notably, not fathers)."
—Lisa Jervis, *Bitch* magazine

Shout Your Abortion

Edited by Amelia Bonow and
Emily Nokes with a Foreword by
Lindy West

ISBN: 978-1-62963-573-6
$24.95   256 pages

Following the U.S. Congress's attempts to
defund Planned Parenthood, the hashtag
#ShoutYourAbortion became a viral conduit for abortion storytelling,
receiving extensive media coverage and positioning real human
experiences at the center of America's abortion debate for the very
first time. The online momentum sparked a grassroots movement that
has subsequently inspired countless individuals to share their abortion
stories in art, media, and community events all over the country, and to
begin building platforms for others to do the same.

Shout Your Abortion is a collection of photos, essays, and creative work
inspired by the movement of the same name, a template for building
new communities of healing, and a call to action. Since SYA's inception,
people all over the country have shared stories and begun organizing
in a range of ways: making art, hosting comedy shows, creating
abortion-positive clothing, altering billboards, starting conversations
that had never happened before. This book documents some of these
projects and illuminates the individuals who have breathed life into this
movement, illustrating the profound liberatory and political power of
defying shame and claiming sole authorship of our experiences. With
Roe vs. Wade on the brink of reversal, the act of shouting one's abortion
has become explicitly radical, and *Shout Your Abortion* is needed more
urgently than ever before.

"Shout Your Abortion *reflects what makes me most hopeful for this next
century, that there's a whole new generation of young people who refuse to
be judged and shamed about who they are, whether it's their gender identity,
their sexual orientation, or what they do with their body.*"
—Cecile Richards, president of Planned Parenthood Federation of
America

"*By presenting a collection of nuanced narratives,* Shout Your Abortion *aims
to advance a message of broader acceptance: If your abortion experience
was hard and sad, that's okay. If your abortion experience wasn't hard or
sad, that's also okay. This marks a significant tonal shift in the cultural
conversation about abortion.*"
—Caitlin Gibson, *Washington Post*

Resistance Behind Bars: The Struggles of Incarcerated Women, 2nd Edition

Victoria Law with an Introduction by Laura Whitehorn

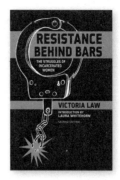

ISBN: 978-1-60486-583-7
$20.00   320 pages

In 1974, women imprisoned at New York's maximum-security prison at Bedford Hills staged what is known as the August Rebellion. Protesting the brutal beating of a fellow prisoner, the women fought off guards, holding seven of them hostage, and took over sections of the prison.

While many have heard of the 1971 Attica prison uprising, the August Rebellion remains relatively unknown even in activist circles. *Resistance Behind Bars* is determined to challenge and change such oversights. As it examines daily struggles against appalling prison conditions and injustices, *Resistance* documents both collective organizing and individual resistance among women incarcerated in the U.S. Emphasizing women's agency in resisting the conditions of their confinement through forming peer education groups, clandestinely arranging ways for children to visit mothers in distant prisons and raising public awareness about their lives, *Resistance* seeks to spark further discussion and research into the lives of incarcerated women and galvanize much-needed outside support for their struggles.

This updated and revised edition of the 2009 PASS Award winning book includes a new chapter about transgender, transsexual, intersex, and gender-variant people in prison.

"Victoria Law's eight years of research and writing, inspired by her unflinching commitment to listen to and support women prisoners, has resulted in an illuminating effort to document the dynamic resistance of incarcerated women in the United States."
— Roxanne Dunbar-Ortiz

"Written in regular English, rather than academese, this is an impressive work of research and reportage"
—Mumia Abu-Jamal, death row political prisoner and author of *Live From Death Row*

Look for Me in the Whirlwind: From the Panther 21 to 21st-Century Revolutions

Sekou Odinga, Dhoruba Bin Wahad, Jamal Joseph
Edited by Matt Meyer & déqui kioni-sadiki with a Foreword by Imam Jamil Al-Amin, and an Afterword by Mumia Abu-Jamal

ISBN: 978-1-62963-389-3
$26.95   648 pages

Amid music festivals and moon landings, the tumultuous year of 1969 included an infamous case in the annals of criminal justice and Black liberation: the New York City Black Panther 21. Though some among the group had hardly even met one another, the 21 were rounded up by the FBI and New York Police Department in an attempt to disrupt and destroy the organization that was attracting young people around the world. Involving charges of conspiracy to commit violent acts, the Panther 21 trial—the longest and most expensive in New York history—revealed the illegal government activities which led to exile, imprisonment on false charges, and assassination of Black liberation leaders. Solidarity for the 21 also extended well beyond "movement" circles and included mainstream publication of their collective autobiography, *Look for Me in the Whirlwind*, which is reprinted here for the first time.

Look for Me in the Whirlwind: From the Panther 21 to 21st-Century Revolutions contains the entire original manuscript, and includes new commentary from surviving members of the 21: Sekou Odinga, Dhoruba Bin Wahad, Jamal Joseph, and Shaba Om. Still-imprisoned Sundiata Acoli, Imam Jamil Al-Amin, and Mumia Abu-Jamal contribute new essays. Never or rarely seen poetry and prose from Afeni Shakur, Kuwasi Balagoon, Ali Bey Hassan, and Michael "Cetewayo" Tabor is included. Early Panther leader and jazz master Bilal Sunni-Ali adds a historical essay and lyrics from his composition "Look for Me in the Whirlwind," and coeditors kioni-sadiki, Meyer, and Panther rank-and-file member Cyril "Bullwhip" Innis Jr. help bring the story up to date.

Report from Planet Midnight

Nalo Hopkinson

ISBN: 978-1-60486-497-7
$12.00   128 pages

Nalo Hopkinson has been busily (and wonderfully) "subverting the genre" since her first novel, *Brown Girl in the Ring*, won a Locus Award for SF and Fantasy in 1999. Since then she has acquired a prestigious World Fantasy Award, a legion of adventurous and aware fans, a reputation for intellect seasoned with humor, and a place of honor in the short list of SF writers who are tearing down the walls of category and transporting readers to previously unimagined planets and realms.

Never one to hold her tongue, Hopkinson takes on sexism and racism in publishing in "Report from Planet Midnight," a historic and controversial presentation to her colleagues and fans.

Plus . . .

"Message in a Bottle," a radical new twist on the time travel tale that demolishes the sentimental myth of childhood innocence; and "Shift," a tempestuous erotic adventure in which Caliban gets the girl. Or does he?

And Featuring: our Outspoken Interview, an intimate one-on-one that delivers a wealth of insight, outrage, irreverence, and top-secret Caribbean spells.

"A genuine vitality and generosity . . . one of the more important and original voices in SF."
—*Publishers Weekly*

"Out-of-the-ordinary science fiction."
—*Kirkus Reviews*

"The plot and style get an early grip on you, the reader, and you don't let go till story's end. Hopkinson is a genuine find!"
—*Locus*

"Hopkinson has had a remarkable impact on popular fiction. Her work continues to question the very genres she adopts, transforming them from within through her fierce intelligence and her commitment to a radical vision that refuses easy consumption."
—*Globe and Mail*